THE SUPPRESSED POEMS
OF
ALFRED LORD TENNYSON
1830–1868

THE SUPPRESSED POEMS

OF

ALFRED LORD TENNYSON

1830-1868

Fredonia Books
Amsterdam, The Netherlands

The Suppressed Poems of Alfred Lord Tennyson
1830-1868

by
J. C. Thomson

ISBN: 1-58963-563-9

Copyright © 2001 by Fredonia Books

Reprinted from the 1910 edition

Fredonia Books
Amsterdam, The Netherlands
http://www.fredoniabooks.com

All rights reserved, including the right to reproduce this book, or portions thereof, in any form.

In order to make original editions of historical works available to scholars at an economical price, this facsimile of the original edition of 1910 is reproduced from the best available copy and has been digitally enhanced to improve legibility, but the text remains unaltered to retain historical authenticity.

Contents

	Page
EDITOR'S NOTE	8
TIMBUCTOO	9
POEMS CHIEFLY LYRICAL	21
i. The How and the Why	23
ii. The Burial of Love	25
iii. To——	27
iv. Song	28
'I' the gloaming light'	
v. Song	29
'Every day hath its night'	
vi. Hero to Leander	31
vii. The Mystic	33
viii. The Grasshopper	35
ix. Love, Pride and Forgetfulness	37
x. Chorus	38
'The varied earth, the moving heaven'	
xi. Lost Hope	40
xii. The Tears of Heaven	41
xiii. Love and Sorrow	42
xiv. To a Lady sleeping	43
xv. Sonnet	44
'Could I outwear my present state of woe'	
xvi. Sonnet	45
'Though night hath climbed'	
xvii. Sonnet	46
'Shall the hag Evil die'	

Contents

                                                                                      Page

POEMS CHIEFLY LYRICAL—*continued*
- xviii. Sonnet 47
  'The pallid thunderstricken sigh for gain'
- xix. Love 48
- xx. English War Song . . . 50
- xxi. National Song 52
- xxii. Dualisms 54
- xxiii. οἱ ῥέοντες 55
- xxiv. Song 56
  'The lintwhite and the throstlecock'

CONTRIBUTIONS TO PERIODICALS, 1831–32 . 59
- xxv. A Fragment 61
- xxvi. Anacreontics 63
- xxvii. 64
  'O sad no more! O sweet no more'
- xxviii. Sonnet 65
  'Check every outflash, every ruder sally'
- xxix. Sonnet 66
  'Me my own fate to lasting sorrow doometh'
- xxx. Sonnet 67
  'There are three things that fill my heart with sighs'

POEMS, 1833 69
- xxxi. Sonnet 71
  'Oh beauty, passing beauty'
- xxxii. The Hesperides . . . 72
- xxxiii. Rosalind 77
- xxxiv. Song 79
  'Who can say'

Contents

	Page
POEMS, 1833—*continued*	
xxxv. Sonnet	80
'*Blow ye the trumpet, gather from afar*'	
xxxvi. O Darling Room	81
xxxvii. To Christopher North	82
xxxviii. The Lotus-Eaters	83
xxxix. A Dream of Fair Women	85
MISCELLANEOUS POEMS AND CONTRIBUTIONS TO PERIODICALS, 1833-68	87
xl. Cambridge	89
xli. The Germ of 'Maud'	90
xlii.	92
'*A gate and a field half ploughed*'	
xliii. The Skipping-rope	93
xliv. The New Timon and the Poets	94
xlv. Mablethorpe	97
xlvi.	98
'*What time I wasted youthful hours*'	
xlvii. Britons, guard your own	99
xlviii. Hands all round	102
xlix. Suggested by reading an article in a newspaper	105
l.	110
'*God bless our Prince and Bride*'	
li. The Ringlet	111
lii. Song	114
'*Home they brought him slain with spears*'	
liii. 1865-1866	115
THE LOVER'S TALE, 1833	117
INDEX OF FIRST LINES	159

Note

To those unacquainted with Tennyson's conscientious methods, it may seem strange that a volume of 160 pages is necessary to contain those poems written and published by him during his active literary career, and ultimately rejected as unsatisfactory. Of this considerable body of verse, a great part was written, not in youth or old age, but while Tennyson's powers were at their greatest. Whatever reasons may once have existed for suppressing the poems that follow, the student of English literature is entitled to demand that the whole body of Tennyson's work should now be open, without restriction or impediment, to the critical study to which the works of his compeers are subjected.

The bibliographical notes prefixed to the various poems give, in every case, the date and medium of first publication.

J. C. T.

Timbuctoo

A POEM

WHICH OBTAINED

THE CHANCELLOR'S MEDAL

AT THE

Cambridge Commencement

MDCCCXXIX

BY

A. TENNYSON

Of Trinity College

[Printed in Cambridge *Chronicle and Journal* of Friday, July 10, 1829, and at the University Press by James Smith, among the *Prolusiones Academicæ Præmiis annuis dignatæ et in Curia Cantabrigiensi Recitatæ Comitiis Maximis*, MDCCCXXIX. Republished in *Cambridge Prize Poems*, 1813 to 1858, by Messrs. Macmillan in 1859, without alteration; and in 1893 in the appendix to a reprint of *Poems by Two Brothers*].

Timbuctoo

> Deep in that lion-haunted inland lies
> A mystic city, goal of high Emprize.
> —Chapman.*

I stood upon the Mountain which o'erlooks
The narrow seas, whose rapid interval
Parts Afric from green Europe, when the Sun
Had fall'n below th' Atlantick, and above
The silent Heavens were blench'd with faery
    light,
Uncertain whether faery light or cloud,
Flowing Southward, and the chasms of deep,
    deep blue
Slumber'd unfathomable, and the stars
Were flooded over with clear glory and pale.
I gaz'd upon the sheeny coast beyond,
There where the Giant of old Time infixed
The limits of his prowess, pillars high
Long time eras'd from Earth : even as the sea
When weary of wild inroad buildeth up
Huge mounds whereby to stay his yeasty waves.
And much I mus'd on legends quaint and old

* Mr Swinburne failed to find this couplet in any of Chapman's original poems or translations, and was of opinion that it is Tennyson's own.

Timbuctoo

Which whilome won the hearts of all on Earth
Toward their brightness, ev'n as flame draws air;
But had their being in the heart of Man
As air is th' life of flame: and thou wert then
A center'd glory-circled Memory,
Divinest Atalantis, whom the waves
Have buried deep, and thou of later name
Imperial Eldorado root'd with gold:
Shadows to which, despite all shocks of Change,
All on-set of capricious Accident,
Men clung with yearning Hope which would not die.

As when in some great City where the walls
Shake, and the streets with ghastly faces throng'd
Do utter forth a subterranean voice,
Among the inner columns far retir'd
At midnight, in the lone Acropolis.
Before the awful Genius of the place
Kneels the pale Priestess in deep faith, the while
Above her head the weak lamp dips and winks
Unto the fearful summoning without:
Nathless she ever clasps the marble knees,
Bathes the cold hand with tears, and gazeth on
Those eyes which wear no light but that wherewith
Her phantasy informs them.

     Where are ye
Thrones of the Western wave, fair Islands green?
Where are your moonlight halls, your cedarn glooms,

Timbuctoo

The blossoming abysses of your hills ?
Your flowering Capes and your gold-sanded bays
Blown round with happy airs of odorous winds ?
Where are the infinite ways which, Seraphtrod,
Wound thro' your great Elysian solitudes,
Whose lowest depths were, as with visible love,
Fill'd with Divine effulgence, circumfus'd,
Flowing between the clear and polish'd stems,
And ever circling round their emerald cones
In coronals and glories, such as gird
The unfading foreheads of the Saints in Heaven ?
For nothing visible, they say, had birth
In that blest ground but it was play'd about
With its peculiar glory. Then I rais'd
My voice and cried 'Wide Afric, doth thy Sun
Lighten, thy hills enfold a City as fair
As those which starr'd the night o' the Elder World?
Or is the rumour of thy Timbuctoo
A dream as frail as those of ancient Time ?'

A curve of whitening, flashing, ebbing light !
A rustling of white wings ! The bright descent
Of a young Seraph ! and he stood beside me
There on the ridge, and look'd into my face
With his unutterable, shining orbs,
So that with hasty motion I did veil
My vision with both hands, and saw before me
Such colour'd spots as dance athwart the eyes
Of those that gaze upon the noonday Sun.
Girt with a Zone of flashing gold beneath
His breast, and compass'd round about his brow

Timbuctoo

With triple arch of everchanging bows,
And circled with the glory of living light
And alternations of all hues, he stood.
'O child of man, why muse you here alone
Upon the Mountain, on the dreams of old
Which fill'd the Earth with passing loveliness,
Which flung strange music on the howling winds
And odours rapt from remote Paradise ?
Thy sense is clogg'd with dull mortality,
Thy spirit fetter'd with the bond of clay :
Open thine eye and see.'

      I look'd, but not
Upon his face, for it was wonderful
With its exceeding brightness, and the light
Of the great angel mind which look'd from out
The starry glowing of his restless eyes.
I felt my soul grow mighty, and my spirit
With supernatural excitation bound
Within me, and my mental eye grew large
With such a vast circumference of thought,
That in my vanity I seem'd to stand
Upon the outward verge and bound alone
Of full beatitude. Each failing sense
As with a momentary flash of light
Grew thrillingly distinct and keen. I saw
The smallest grain that dappled the dark Earth,
The indistinctest atom in deep air,
The Moon's white cities, and the opal width
Of her small glowing lakes, her silver heights
Unvisited with dew of vagrant cloud,

Timbuctoo

And the unsounded, undescended depth
Of her black hollows. The clear Galaxy
Shorn of its hoary lustre, wonderful,
Distinct and vivid with sharp points of light
Blaze within blaze, an unimagin'd depth
And harmony of planet-girded Suns
And moon-encircled planets, wheel in wheel,
Arch'd the wan Sapphire. Nay, the hum of men,
Or other things talking in unknown tongues,
And notes of busy life in distant worlds
Beat like a far wave on my anxious ear.

A maze of piercing, trackless, thrilling thoughts
Involving and embracing each with each
Rapid as fire, inextricably link'd,
Expanding momently with every sight
And sound which struck the palpitating sense,
The issue of strong impulse, hurried through
The riv'n rapt brain : as when in some large lake
From pressure of descendant crags, which lapse
Disjointed, crumbling from their parent slope
At slender interval, the level calm
Is ridg'd with restless and increasing spheres
Which break upon each other, each th' effect
Of separate impulse, but more fleet and strong
Than its precursor, till the eyes in vain
Amid the wild unrest of swimming shade
Dappled with hollow and alternate rise
Of interpenetrated arc, would scan
Definite round.
                I know not if I shape

Timbuctoo

These things with accurate similitude
From visible objects, for but dimly now,
Less vivid than a half-forgotten dream,
The memory of that mental excellence
Comes o'er me, and it may be I entwine
The indecision of my present mind
With its past clearness, yet it seems to me
As even then the torrent of quick thought
Absorbed me from the nature of itself
With its own fleetness. Where is he that, borne
Adown the sloping of an arrowy stream,
Could link his shallop to the fleeting edge,
And muse midway with philosophic calm
Upon the wondrous laws which regulate
The fierceness of the bounding element?
My thoughts which long had grovell'd in the slime
Of this dull world, like dusky worms which house
Beneath unshaken waters, but at once
Upon some earth-awakening day of spring
Do pass from gloom to glory, and aloft
Winnow the purple, bearing on both sides
Double display of starlit wings which burn
Fanlike and fibred, with intensest bloom:
E'en so my thoughts, erewhile so low, now felt
Unutterable buoyancy and strength
To bear them upward through the trackless fields
Of undefin'd existence far and free.

Then first within the South methought I saw
A wilderness of spires, and chrystal pile
Of rampart upon rampart, dome on dome,

Timbuctoo

Illimitable range of battlement
On battlement, and the Imperial height
Of Canopy o'ercanopied.
                        Behind,
In diamond light, upsprung the dazzling Cones
Of Pyramids, as far surpassing Earth's
As Heaven than Earth is fairer. Each aloft
Upon his renown'd Eminence bore globes
Of wheeling suns, or stars, or semblances
Of either, showering circular abyss
Of radiance. But the glory of the place
Stood out a pillar'd front of burnish'd gold
Interminably high, if gold it were
Or metal more ethereal, and beneath
Two doors of blinding brilliance, where no gaze
Might rest, stood open, and the eye could scan
Through length of porch and lake and boundless
    hall,
Part of a throne of fiery flame, wherefrom
The snowy skirting of a garment hung,
And glimpse of multitudes of multitudes
That minister'd around it—if I saw
These things distinctly, for my human brain
Stagger'd beneath the vision, and thick night
Came down upon my eyelids, and I fell.

With ministering hand he rais'd me up;
Then with a mournful and ineffable smile,
Which but to look on for a moment fill'd
My eyes with irresistible sweet tears,
In accents of majestic melody,

Timbuctoo

Like a swol'n river's gushings in still night
Mingled with floating music, thus he spake :
'There is no mightier Spirit than I to sway
The heart of man : and teach him to attain
By shadowing forth the Unattainable ;
And step by step to scale that mighty stair
Whose landing-place is wrapt about with clouds
Of glory of Heaven.* With earliest Light of
    Spring,
And in the glow of sallow Summertide,
And in red Autumn when the winds are wild
With gambols, and when full-voiced Winter roofs
The headland with inviolate white snow,
I play about his heart a thousand ways,
Visit his eyes with visions, and his ears
With harmonies of wind and wave and wood
—Of winds which tell of waters, and of waters
Betraying the close kisses of the wind—
And win him unto me : and few there be
So gross of heart who have not felt and known
A higher than they see : They with dim eyes
Behold me darkling. Lo ! I have given *thee*
To understand my presence, and to feel
My fullness ; I have fill'd thy lips with power.
I have rais'd thee higher to the Spheres of Heaven,
Man's first, last home : and thou with ravish'd
    sense
Listenest the lordly music flowing from

---

* Be ye perfect even as your Father in Heaven is perfect.

Timbuctoo

Th' illimitable years. I am the Spirit,
The permeating life which courseth through
All th' intricate and labyrinthine veins
Of the great vine of *Fable*, which, outspread
With growth of shadowing leaf and clusters rare,
Reacheth to every corner under Heaven,
Deep-rooted in the living soil of truth :
So that men's hopes and fears take refuge in
The fragrance of its complicated glooms
And cool impleachèd twilights. Child of Man,
See'st thou yon river, whose translucent wave,
Forth issuing from darkness, windeth through
The argent streets o' the City, imaging
The soft inversion of her tremulous Domes ;
Her gardens frequent with the stately Palm,
Her Pagods hung with music of sweet bells :
Her obelisks of rangèd Chrysolite,
Minarets and towers ? Lo ! how he passeth by,
And gulphs himself in sands, as not enduring
To carry through the world those waves, which bore
The reflex of my City in their depths.
Oh City ! Oh latest Throne ! where I was rais'd
To be a mystery of loveliness
Unto all eyes, the time is well nigh come
When I must render up this glorious home
To keen *Discovery* : soon yon brilliant towers
Shall darken with the waving of her wand ;
Darken, and shrink and shiver into huts,
Black specks amid a waste of dreary sand,
Low-built, mud-walled, Barbarian settlement,
How chang'd from this fair City !'

Timbuctoo

                Thus far the Spirit :
Then parted Heavenward on the wing : and I
Was left alone on Calpe, and the Moon
Had fallen from the night, and all was dark !

[The following review of 'Timbuctoo' was published in the *Athenæum* of 22nd July, 1829: 'We have accustomed ourselves to think, perhaps without any very good reason, that poetry was likely to perish among us for a considerable period after the great generation of poets which is now passing away. The age seems determined to contradict us, and that in the most decided manner; for it has put forth poetry by a young man, and that where we should least expect it—namely, in a prize poem These productions have often been ingenious and elegant but we have never before seen one of them which indicated really first-rate poetical genius, and which would have done honour to any men that ever wrote. Such, we do not hesitate to affirm, is the little work before us; and the examiners seem to have felt it like ourselves, for they have assigned the prize to the author, though the measure in which he writes was never before, we believe, thus selected for honour. We extract a few lines to justify our admiration (50 lines, 62-112, quoted). How many men have lived for a century who could equal this?' At the time when this highly eulogistic notice of the youthful unknown poet appeared, the *Athenæum* was edited by John Sterling and Frederick Denison Maurice, its then proprietors.]

Poems Chiefly Lyrical

[The poems numbered I-XXIV which follow, were published in 1830 in the volume *Poems chiefly Lyrical*. (London: Effingham Wilson, Royal Exchange, 1830.) They were never republished by Tennyson.]

Poems Chiefly Lyrical

I

The 'How' and the 'Why'

    I am any man's suitor,
       If any will be my tutor :
Some say this life is pleasant,
       Some think it speedeth fast :
In time there is no present,
       In eternity no future,
       In eternity no past.
We laugh, we cry, we are born, we die,
Who will riddle me the *how* and the *why* ?

The bulrush nods unto his brother
The wheatears whisper to each other :
What is it they say ?   What do they there ?
Why two and two make four ? Why round is not square ?
Why the rocks stand still, and the light clouds fly ?
Why the heavy oak groans, and the white willows sigh ?
Why deep is not high, and high is not deep ?
Whether we wake or whether we sleep ?
Whether we sleep or whether we die ?
How you are you ?   Why I am I ?
Who will riddle me the *how* and the *why* ?

Poems Chiefly Lyrical

The world is somewhat ; it goes on somehow ;
But what is the meaning of *then* and *now* !
I feel there is something ; but how and what ?
I know there is somewhat ; but what and why !
I cannot tell if that somewhat be I.

The little bird pipeth 'why ! why !'
In the summerwoods when the sun falls low,
And the great bird sits on the opposite bough,
And stares in his face and shouts 'how ? how ?'
And the black owl scuds down the mellow twilight
And chaunts 'how ? how ?' the whole of the night

Why the life goes when the blood is spilt ?
What the life is ? where the soul may lie ?
Why a church is with a steeple built ;
And a house with a chimney-pot ?
Who will riddle me the how and the what ?
Who will riddle me the what and the why ?

Poems Chiefly Lyrical

II

The Burial of Love

His eyes in eclipse,
    Pale cold his lips,
The light of his hopes unfed,
    Mute his tongue,
    His bow unstrung
With the tears he hath shed,
Backward drooping his graceful head.

    Love is dead ;
    His last arrow sped ;
He hath not another dart ;
    Go—carry him to his dark deathbed ;
Bury him in the cold, cold heart—
    Love is dead.

Oh, truest love ! art thou forlorn,
    And unrevenged ? Thy pleasant wiles
Forgotten, and thine innocent joy ?
    Shall hollow-hearted apathy,
The cruellest form of perfect scorn,
    With langour of most hateful smiles,
For ever write
In the weathered light
    Of the tearless eye
    An epitaph that all may spy ?
    No ! sooner she herself shall die.

Poems Chiefly Lyrical

For her the showers shall not fall,
Nor the round sun that shineth to all;
   Her light shall into darkness change;
For her the green grass shall not spring,
Nor the rivers flow, nor the sweet birds sing
   Till Love have his full revenge.

Poems Chiefly Lyrical

III
To——

Sainted Juliet! dearest name!
    If to love be life alone,
      Divinest Juliet,
    I love thee, and live; and yet
Love unreturned is like the fragrant flame
    Folding the slaughter of the sacrifice
    Offered to Gods upon an altarthrone;
My heart is lighted at thine eyes,
Changed into fire, and blown about with sighs

Poems Chiefly Lyrical

IV

Song

I

    I' the glooming light
    Of middle night,
    So cold and white,
Worn Sorrow sits by the moaning wave;
      Beside her are laid,
      Her mattock and spade,
For she hath half delved her own deep grave.
    Alone she is there:
The white clouds drizzle: her hair falls loose;
      Her shoulders are bare;
Her tears are mixed with the bearded dews.

II

    Death standeth by;
    She will not die;
    With glazèd eye
She looks at her grave: she cannot sleep;
      Ever alone
      She maketh her moan:
She cannot speak; she can only weep;
    For she will not hope.
The thick snow falls on her flake by flake,
    The dull wave mourns down the slope,
The world will not change, and her heart will not break.

Poems Chiefly Lyrical

V
Song

I

Every day hath its night :
    Every night its morn :
Through dark and bright
    Wingèd hours are borne ;
      Ah ! welaway !
Seasons flower and fade ;
    Golden calm and storm
      Mingle day by day.
    There is no bright form
Doth not cast a shade—
      Ah ! welaway !

II

When we laugh, and our mirth
    Apes the happy vein,
We're so kin to earth
    Pleasuance fathers pain—
      Ah ! welaway !
Madness laugheth loud :
    Laughter bringeth tears :
      Eyes are worn away
    Till the end of fears
Cometh in the shroud,
      Ah ! welaway !

Poems Chiefly Lyrical

III

All is change, woe or weal;
    Joy is sorrow's brother;
Grief and sadness steal
    Symbols of each other;
        Ah! welaway!
Larks in heaven's cope
    Sing: the culvers mourn
        All the livelong day
Be not all forlorn;
Let us weep in hope—
        Ah! welaway!

Poems Chiefly Lyrical

VI

Hero to Leander

Oʜ go not yet, my love,
    The night is dark and vast;
The white moon is hid in her heaven above,
    And the waves climb high and fast.
Oh! kiss me, kiss me, once again,
    Lest thy kiss should be the last.
    Oh kiss me ere we part;
    Grow closer to my heart.
My heart is warmer surely than the bosom of the
    main.

Oh joy! O bliss of blisses!
    My heart of hearts art thou.
Come bathe me with thy kisses,
    My eyelids and my brow.
Hark how the wild rain hisses,
    And the loud sea roars below.

Thy heart beats through thy rosy limbs
    So gladly doth it stir;
Thine eye in drops of gladness swims.
    I have bathed thee with the pleasant myrrh;

Poems Chiefly Lyrical

Thy locks are dripping balm ;
    Thou shalt not wander hence to-night,
I'll stay thee with my kisses.
    To-night the roaring brine
Will rend thy golden tresses ;
    The ocean with the morrow light
Will be both blue and calm ;
    And the billow will embrace thee with a kiss
        as soft as mine.

No western odours wander
    On the black and moaning sea,
And when thou art dead, Leander,
    My soul shall follow thee !
Oh go not yet, my love,
    Thy voice is sweet and low ;
The deep salt wave breaks in above
    Those marble steps below.
The turretstairs are wet
    That lead into the sea.
Leander ! go not yet.
The pleasant stars have set !
Oh ! go not, go not yet,
    Or I will follow thee.

Poems Chiefly Lyrical

VII

The Mystic

ANGELS have talked with him, and showed him
    thrones:
Ye knew him not: he was not one of ye,
Ye scorned him with an undiscerning scorn:
Ye could not read the marvel in his eye,
The still serene abstraction; he hath felt
The vanities of after and before;
Albeit, his spirit and his secret heart
The stern experiences of converse lives,
The linkèd woes of many a fiery change
Had purified, and chastened, and made free.
Always there stood before him, night and day,
Of wayward vary coloured circumstance,
The imperishable presences serene,
Colossal, without form, or sense, or sound,
Dim shadows but unwaning presences
Fourfacèd to four corners of the sky;
And yet again, three shadows, fronting one,
One forward, one respectant, three but one;
And yet again, again and evermore,
For the two first were not, but only seemed
One shadow in the midst of a great light,

Poems Chiefly Lyrical

One reflex from eternity on time,
One mighty countenance of perfect calm,
Awful with most invariable eyes.
For him the silent congregated hours,
Daughters of time, divinely tall, beneath
Severe and youthful brows, with shining eyes
Smiling a godlike smile (the innocent light
Of earliest youth pierced through and through
    with all
Keen knowledges of low-embowèd eld)
Upheld, and ever hold aloft the cloud
Which droops low hung on either gate of life,
Both birth and death ; he in the centre fixed,
Saw far on each side through the grated gates
Most pale and clear and lovely distances.
He often lying broad awake, and yet
Remaining from the body, and apart
In intellect and power and will, hath heard
Time flowing in the middle of the night,
And all things creeping to a day of doom.
How could ye know him ? Ye were yet within
The narrower circle ; he had well nigh reached
The last, with which a region of white flame,
Pure without heat, into a larger air
Upburning, and an ether of black hue,
Investeth and ingirds all other lives.

Poems Chiefly Lyrical

VIII
The Grasshopper

1

Voice of the summerwind,
    Joy of the summerplain,
    Life of the summerhours,
  Carol clearly, bound along.
  No Tithon thou as poets feign
(Shame fall 'em they are deaf and blind)
    But an insect lithe and strong,
      Bowing the seeded summerflowers.
Prove their falsehood and thy quarrel,
    Vaulting on thine airy feet.
Clap thy shielded sides and carol,
    Carol clearly, chirrup sweet
Thou art a mailèd warrior in youth and strength
      complete ;
    Armed cap-a-pie,
    Full fair to see ;
      Unknowing fear,
      Undreading loss,
      A gallant cavalier
Sans peur et sans reproche,
    In sunlight and in shadow,
    The Bayard of the meadow.

Poems Chiefly Lyrical

II

I would dwell with thee,
    Merry grasshopper,
Thou art so glad and free,
    And as light as air ;
Thou hast no sorrow or tears,
Thou hast no compt of years,
No withered immortality,
But a short youth sunny and free.
Carol clearly, bound along,
    Soon thy joy is over,
A summer of loud song,
    And slumbers in the clover.
    What hast thou to do with evil
    In thine hour of love and revel,
    In thy heat of summerpride,
    Pushing the thick roots aside
    Of the singing flowerèd grasses,
    That brush thee with their silken tresses ?
What hast thou to do with evil,
Shooting, singing, ever springing
    In and out the emerald glooms,
Ever leaping, ever singing,
    Lighting on the golden blooms ?

Poems Chiefly Lyrical

IX

Love, Pride and Forgetfulness

Ere yet my heart was sweet Love's tomb,
Love laboured honey busily.
I was the hive and Love the bee,
My heart the honey-comb.
One very dark and chilly night
Pride came beneath and held a light.

The cruel vapours went through all,
Sweet Love was withered in his cell;
Pride took Love's sweets, and by a spell
Did change them into gall;
And Memory tho' fed by Pride
Did wax so thin on gall,
Awhile she scarcely lived at all,
What marvel that she died?

Poems Chiefly Lyrical

X

Chorus

In an unpublished drama written very early

The varied earth, the moving heaven,
    The rapid waste of roving sea,
The fountainpregnant mountains riven
    To shapes of wildest anarchy,
By secret fire and midnight storms
    That wander round their windy cones
The subtle life, the countless forms
    Of living things, the wondrous tones
Of man and beast are full of strange
Astonishment and boundless change.

The day, the diamonded light,
    The echo, feeble child of sound,
The heavy thunder's girding might,
    The herald lightning's starry bound,
The vocal spring of bursting bloom,
    The naked summer's glowing birth,
The troublous autumn's sallow gloom,
    The hoarhead winter paving earth
With sheeny white, are full of strange
Astonishment and boundless change.

Poems Chiefly Lyrical

Each sun which from the centre flings
    Grand music and redundant fire,
The burning belts, the mighty rings,
    The murmurous planets' rolling choir
The globefilled arch that, cleaving air,
    Lost in its effulgence sleeps,
The lawless comets as they glare,
    And thunder thro' the sapphire deeps
In wayward strength, are full of strange
Astonishment and boundless change.

Poems Chiefly Lyrical

XI

Lost Hope

You cast to ground the hope which once was
>   mine,
>   But did the while your harsh decree deplore,
Embalming with sweet tears the vacant shrine,
>   My heart, where Hope had been and was
>   no more.

So on an oaken sprout
>   A goodly acorn grew;
But winds from heaven shook the acorn out,
>   And filled the cup with dew.

Poems Chiefly Lyrical

XII

The Tears of Heaven

HEAVEN weeps above the earth all night till morn,
In darkness weeps, as all ashamed to weep,
Because the earth hath made her state forlorn
With selfwrought evils of unnumbered years,
And doth the fruit of her dishonour reap.
And all the day heaven gathers back her tears
Into her own blue eyes so clear and deep,
And showering down the glory of lightsome day,
Smiles on the earth's worn brow to win her if
    she may.

Poems Chiefly Lyrical

XIII

Love and Sorrow

O Maiden, fresher than the first green leaf
With which the fearful springtide flecks the lea,
Weep not, Almeida, that I said to thee
That thou hast half my heart, for bitter grief
Doth hold the other half in sovranty.
Thou art my heart's sun in love's crystalline:
Yet on both sides at once thou canst not shine:
Thine is the bright side of my heart, and thine
My heart's day, but the shadow of my heart,
Issue of its own substance, my heart's night
Thou canst not lighten even with *thy* light,
All powerful in beauty as thou art.
Almeida, if my heart were substanceless,
Then might thy rays pass thro' to the other side,
So swiftly, that they nowhere would abide,
But lose themselves in utter emptiness.
Half-light, half-shadow, let my spirit sleep
They never learnt to love who never knew to weep.

Poems Chiefly Lyrical

XIV

To a Lady Sleeping

O thou whose fringèd lids I gaze upon,
Through whose dim brain the wingèd dreams are born,
Unroof the shrines of clearest vision,
In honour of the silverfleckèd morn:
Long hath the white wave of the virgin light
Driven back the billow of the dreamful dark.
Thou all unwittingly prolongest night,
Though long ago listening the poisèd lark,
With eyes dropt downward through the blue serene,
Over heaven's parapets the angels lean.

Poems Chiefly Lyrical

XV

Sonnet

Could I outwear my present state of woe
With one brief winter, and indue i' the spring
Hues of fresh youth, and mightily outgrow
The wan dark coil of faded suffering—
Forth in the pride of beauty issuing
A sheeny snake, the light of vernal bowers,
Moving his crest to all sweet plots of flowers
And watered vallies where the young birds sing
Could I thus hope my lost delights renewing,
I straightly would commend the tears to creep
From my charged lids; but inwardly I weep:
Some vital heat as yet my heart is wooing:
This to itself hath drawn the frozen rain
From my cold eyes and melted it again.

Poems Chiefly Lyrical

XVI

Sonnet

Though Night hath climbed her peak of highest noon,
And bitter blasts the screaming autumn whirl,
All night through archways of the bridgèd pearl
And portals of pure silver walks the moon.
Wake on, my soul, nor crouch to agony :
Turn cloud to light, and bitterness to joy,
And dross to gold with glorious alchemy,
Basing thy throne above the world's annoy.
Reign thou above the storms of sorrow and ruth
That roar beneath ; unshaken peace hath won thee :
So shalt thou pierce the woven glooms of truth ;
So shall the blessing of the meek be on thee ;
So in thine hour of dawn, the body's youth,
An honourable eld shall come upon thee.

Poems Chiefly Lyrical

XVII

Sonnet

Shall the hag Evil die with the child of Good,
Or propagate again her loathèd kind,
Thronging the cells of the diseased mind,
Hateful with hanging cheeks, a withered brood,
Though hourly pastured on the salient blood?
Oh! that the wind which bloweth cold or heat
Would shatter and o'erbear the brazen beat
Of their broad vans, and in the solitude
Of middle space confound them, and blow back
Their wild cries down their cavernthroats, and slake
With points of blastborne hail their heated eyne!
So their wan limbs no more might come between
The moon and the moon's reflex in the night;
Nor blot with floating shades the solar light.

Poems Chiefly Lyrical

XVIII

Sonnet

THE palid thunderstricken sigh for gain,
Down an ideal stream they ever float,
And sailing on Pactolus in a boat,
Drown soul and sense, while wistfully they strain
Weak eyes upon the glistering sands that robe
The understream. The wise could he behold
Cathedralled caverns of thick-ribbèd gold
And branching silvers of the central globe,
Would marvel from so beautiful a sight
How scorn and ruin, pain and hate could flow:
But Hatred in a gold cave sits below,
Pleached with her hair, in mail of argent light
Shot into gold, a snake her forehead clips
And skins the colour from her trembling lips.

Poems Chiefly Lyrical

XIX

Love

I

Thou, from the first, unborn, undying love,
Albeit we gaze not on thy glories near,
Before the face of God didst breath and move,
Though night and pain and ruin and death reign
    here.
Thou foldest, like a golden atmosphere,
The very throne of the eternal God :
Passing through thee the edicts of his fear
Are mellowed into music, borne abroad
By the loud winds, though they uprend the sea,
Even from his central deeps : thine empery
Is over all : thou wilt not brook eclipse ;
Thou goest and returnest to His Lips
Like lightning : thou dost ever brood above
The silence of all hearts, unutterable Love.

II

To know thee is all wisdom, and old age
Is but to know thee : dimly we behold thee
Athwart the veils of evil which enfold thee
We beat upon our aching hearts with rage ;
We cry for thee : we deem the world thy tomb.

Poems Chiefly Lyrical

As dwellers in lone planets look upon
The mighty disk of their majestic sun,
Hallowed in awful chasms of wheeling gloom,
Making their day dim, so we gaze on thee.
Come, thou of many crowns, white-robèd love,
Oh ! rend the veil in twain : all men adore thee
Heaven crieth after thee ; earth waileth for thee
Breathe on thy wingèd throne, and it shall move
In music and in light o'er land and sea.

III

And now—methinks I gaze upon thee now,
As on a serpent in his agonies
Awestricken Indians ; what time laid low
And crushing the thick fragrant reeds he lies,
When the new year warm breathèd on the earth,
Waiting to light him with his purple skies,
Calls to him by the fountain to uprise.
Already with the pangs of a new birth
Strain the hot spheres of his convulsèd eyes,
And in his writhings awful hues begin
To wander down his sable sheeny sides,
Like light on troubled waters : from within
Anon he rusheth forth with merry din,
And in him light and joy and strength abides ;
And from his brows a crown of living light
Looks through the thickstemmed woods by day
    and night

Poems Chiefly Lyrical

XX

English War Song

Who fears to die ? Who fears to die ?
  Is there any here who fears to die
He shall find what he fears, and none shall grieve
  For the man who fears to die :
But the withering scorn of the many shall cleave
  To the man who fears to die.

  Chorus.—Shout for England !
      Ho ! for England !
      George for England !
      Merry England !
      England for aye !

The hollow at heart shall crouch forlorn,
He shall eat the bread of common scorn ;
  It shall be steeped in the salt, salt tear,
  Shall be steeped in his own salt tear :
Far better, far better he never were born
  Than to shame merry England here.

  Chorus.—Shout for England ! *etc.*

Poems Chiefly Lyrical

There standeth our ancient enemy ;
Hark ! he shouteth—the ancient enemy !
    On the ridge of the hill his banners rise ;
    They stream like fire in the skies ;
Hold up the Lion of England on high
    Till it dazzle and blind his eyes.

    Chorus.—Shout for England ! *etc.*

Come along ! we alone of the earth are free ;
The child in our cradles is bolder than he ;
    For where is the heart and strength of slaves ?
    Oh ! where is the strength of slaves ?
He is weak ! we are strong ; he a slave, we are free ;
    Come along ! we will dig their graves.

    Chorus.—Shout for England ! *etc.*

There standeth our ancient enemy ;
Will he dare to battle with the free ?
    Spur along ! spur amain ! charge to the fight :
    Charge ! charge to the fight !
Hold up the Lion of England on high !
    Shout for God and our right !

    Chorus.—Shout for England ! *etc.*

Poems Chiefly Lyrical

XXI

National Song

THERE is no land like England
  Where'er the light of day be;
There are no hearts like English hearts,
  Such hearts of oak as they be.
There is no land like England
  Where'er the light of day be;
There are no men like Englishmen,
  So tall and bold as they be.

Chorus.—For the French the Pope may shrive 'em
  For the devil a whit we heed 'em,
As for the French, God speed 'em
  Unto their hearts' desire,
And the merry devil drive 'em
  Through the water and the fire.

Chorus.—Our glory is our freedom,
  We lord it o'er the sea;
We are the sons of freedom,
  We are free.

Poems Chiefly Lyrical

There is no land like England,
　Where'er the light of day be ;
There are no wives like English wives,
　So fair and chaste as they be.
There is no land like England,
　Where'er the light of day be,
There are no maids like English maids,
　So beautiful as they be.

Chorus.—For the French, *etc.*

[Sixty years after first publication this Song was incorporated in 'The Foresters' (published 1892) as the opening chorus of the second act. The two verses were unaltered, but the two choruses were re-written.]

Poems Chiefly Lyrical

XXII

Dualisms

Two bees within a chrystal flowerbell rockèd
Hum a lovelay to the westwind at noontide.
Both alike, they buzz together,
Both alike, they hum together
Through and through the flowered heather.

Where in a creeping cove the wave unshockèd
   Lays itself calm and wide,
Over a stream two birds of glancing feather
Do woo each other, carolling together.
Both alike, they glide together
   Side by side ;
Both alike, they sing together,
Arching blue-glossèd necks beneath the purple weather.

Two children lovelier than love, adown the lea are singing,
As they gambol, lilygarlands ever stringing :
Both in blosmwhite silk are frockèd :
Like, unlike, they roam together
Under a summervault of golden weather ;
Like, unlike, they sing together
   Side by side ;
Mid May's darling goldenlockèd,
Summer's tanling diamondeyed.

Poems Chiefly Lyrical

XXIII

οἱ ῥέοντες

I

ALL thoughts, all creeds, all dreams are true,
　All visions wild and strange;
Man is the measure of all truth
　Unto himself. All truth is change:
All men do walk in sleep, and all
　Have faith in that they dream:
For all things are as they seem to all,
　And all things flow like a stream.

II

There is no rest, no calm, no pause,
　Nor good nor ill, nor light nor shade,
Nor essence nor eternal laws:
　For nothing is, but all is made,
But if I dream that all these are,
　They are to me for that I dream;
For all things are as they seem to all,
　And all things flow like a stream.

Argal.—This very opinion is only true relatively to the flowing philosophers. (Tennyson's note.)

Poems Chiefly Lyrical

XXIV

Song

I

The lintwhite and the throstlecock
  Have voices sweet and clear;
 All in the bloomèd May.
They from the blosmy brere
Call to the fleeting year,
If that he would them hear
   And stay.
Alas! that one so beautiful
  Should have so dull an ear.

II

Fair year, fair year, thy children call
  But thou art deaf as death;
 All in the bloomèd May.
When thy light perisheth
That from thee issueth,
Our life evanisheth:
   Oh! stay.
Alas! that lips so cruel dumb
  Should have so sweet a breath!

Poems Chiefly Lyrical

III

Fair year, with brows of royal love
    Thou comest, as a King.
  All in the bloomèd May.
Thy golden largess fling,
And longer hear us sing;
Though thou art fleet of wing,
    Yet stay.
Alas! that eyes so full of light
  Should be so wandering!

IV

Thy locks are full of sunny sheen
    In rings of gold yronne,*
  All in the bloomèd May,
We pri'·thee pass not on;
If thou dost leave the sun,
Delight is with thee gone,
    Oh! stay.
Thou art the fairest of thy feres,
  We pri' thee pass not on.

---

* His crispè hair in ringis was yronne.—Chaucer *Knight's Tale*. (Tennyson's note.)

Contributions to Periodicals
1831-2

Contributions to Periodicals

XXV

A Fragment

[Published in *The Gem : a Literary Annual*. London :
W. Marshall, Holborn Bars. mdcccxxxi.]

WHERE is the Giant of the Sun, which stood
In the midnoon the glory of old Rhodes,
A perfect Idol, with profulgent brows
Far sheening down the purple seas to those
Who sailed from Mizraim underneath the star
Named of the Dragon—and between whose limbs
Of brassy vastness broad-blown Argosies
Drave into haven ? Yet endure unscathed
Of changeful cycles the great Pyramids
Broad-based amid the fleeting sands, and sloped
Into the slumberous summer noon ; but where,
Mysterious Egypt, are thine obelisks
Graven with gorgeous emblems undiscerned ?
Thy placid Sphinxes brooding o'er the Nile ?
Thy shadowy Idols in the solitudes,
Awful Memnonian countenances calm
Looking athwart the burning flats, far off
Seen by the high-necked camel on the verge

Contributions to Periodicals

Journeying southward ? Where are thy monuments
Piled by the strong and sunborn Anakim
Over their crowned brethren O<small>N</small> and O<small>PH</small> ?
Thy Memnon, when his peaceful lips are kissed
With earliest rays, that from his mother's eyes
Flow over the Arabian bay, no more
Breathes low into the charmed ears of morn
Clear melody flattering the crisped Nile
By columned Thebes. Old Memphis hath gone down :
The Pharaohs are no more : somewhere in death
They sleep with staring eyes and gilded lips,
Wrapped round with spiced cerements in old grots
Rock-hewn and sealed for ever.

Contributions to Periodicals

XXVI

Anacreontics

[Published in *The Gem: a Literary Annual*. London
W. Marshall, Holborn Bars. mdcccxxxi.]

WITH roses musky breathed,
And drooping daffodilly,
And silverleaved lily,
And ivy darkly-wreathed,
I wove a crown before her,
For her I love so dearly,
A garland for Lenora.
With a silken cord I bound it.
Lenora, laughing clearly
A light and thrilling laughter,
About her forehead wound it,
And loved me ever after.

Contributions to Periodicals

XXVII

[Published in *The Gem: a Literary Annual*. London
W. Marshall, Holborn Bars. mdcccxxxi.]

O SAD *No more!* O sweet *No more!*
   O strange *No more!*
By a mossed brookbank on a stone
I smelt a wildweed flower alone;
There was a ringing in my ears,
   And both my eyes gushed out with tears.
Surely all pleasant things had gone before,
Low-buried fathom deep beneath with thee,

   NO MORE!

Contributions to Periodicals

XXVIII

Sonnet

[Published in the *Englishman's Magazine*, August, 1831.
London: Edward Moxon, 64 New Bond Street.
Reprinted in *Friendship's Offering: a Literary
Album* for 1833. London; Smith and Elder.]

CHECK every outflash, every ruder sally
    Of thought and speech; speak low, and give up
        wholly
    Thy spirit to mild-minded Melancholy;
This is the place. Through yonder poplar alley
Below, the blue-green river windeth slowly;
    But in the middle of the sombre valley
    The crispèd waters whisper musically,
And all the haunted place is dark and holy.
The nightingale, with long and low preamble,
    Warbled from yonder knoll of solemn larches,
    And in and out the woodbine's flowery arches
The summer midges wove their wanton gambol,
    And all the white-stemmed pinewood slept
        above—
When in this valley first I told my love.

Contributions to Periodicals

XXIX

Sonnet

[Published in *Friendship's Offering: a Literary Album* for 1832. London: Smith and Elder.]

ME my own fate to lasting sorrow doometh:
   Thy woes are birds of passage, transitory:
   Thy spirit, circled with a living glory,
In summer still a summer joy resumeth.
Alone my hopeless melancholy gloometh,
   Like a lone cypress, through the twilight hoary,
From an old garden where no flower bloometh,
   One cypress on an inland promontory.
But yet my lonely spirit follows thine,
   As round the rolling earth night follows day:
But yet thy lights on my horizon shine
   Into my night when thou art far away;
I am so dark, alas! and thou so bright,
When we two meet there's never perfect light.

Contributions to Periodicals

XXX

Sonnet

[Published in the *Yorkshire Literary Annual* for 1832. Edited by C. F. Edgar. London: Longman and Co. Reprinted in the *Athenæum*, 4 May, 1867.]

THERE are three things that fill my heart with sighs
And steep my soul in laughter (when I view
Fair maiden forms moving like melodies),
Dimples, roselips, and eyes of any hue.

There are three things beneath the blessed skies
For which I live—black eyes, and brown and blue;
I hold them all most dear; but oh! black eyes,
I live and die, and only die for you.

Of late such eyes looked at me—while I mused
At sunset, underneath a shadowy plane
In old Bayona, nigh the Southern Sea—
From an half-open lattice looked at *me*.

I saw no more only those eyes—confused
And dazzled to the heart with glorious pain.

Poems, 1833

[The poems numbered XXXI-XXXIX were published in the 1832 volume (*Poems by Alfred Tennyson*. London: Edward Moxon, 94 New Bond Street. MDCCCXXXIII; published December, 1832), and were thereafter suppressed.]

Poems, 1833

XXXI

Sonnet

Oh, Beauty, passing beauty! sweetest Sweet!
  How canst thou let me waste my youth in sighs
I only ask to sit beside thy feet.
  Thou knowest I dare not look into thine eyes
Might I but kiss thy hand! I dare not fold
  My arms about thee—scarcely dare to speak.
And nothing seems to me so wild and bold,
  As with one kiss to touch thy blessèd cheek.
Methinks if I should kiss thee, no control
  Within the thrilling brain could keep afloat
  The subtle spirit. Even while I spoke,
The bare word KISS hath made my inner soul
  To tremble like a lutestring, ere the note
  Hath melted in the silence that it broke.

Poems, 1833

XXXII

The Hesperides

> Hesperus and his daughters three
> That sing about the golden tree.
> —Comus.

The Northwind fall'n, in the newstarréd night
Zidonian Hanno, voyaging beyond
The hoary promontory of Soloë
Past Thymiaterion, in calmèd bays,
Between the Southern and the Western Horn,
Heard neither warbling of the nightingale,
Nor melody o' the Lybian lotusflute
Blown seaward from the shore; but from a slope
That ran bloombright into the Atlantic blue,
Beneath a highland leaning down a weight
Of cliffs, and zoned below with cedarshade,
Came voices, like the voices in a dream,
Continuous till he reached the other sea.

Song

I

The golden apple, the golden apple, the hallowed fruit,
Guard it well, guard it warily,
Singing airily,
Standing about the charméd root.
Round about all is mute,

Poems, 1833

As the snowfield on the mountain-peaks,
As the sandfield at the mountain-foot.
Crocodiles in briny creeks
Sleep and stir not : all is mute.
If ye sing not, if ye make false measure,
We shall lose eternal pleasure,
Worth eternal want of rest.
Laugh not loudly : watch the treasure
Of the wisdom of the West.
In a corner wisdom whispers. Five and three
(Let it not be preached abroad) make an awful
    mystery.
For the blossom unto three-fold music bloweth ;
Evermore it is born anew ;
And the sap to three-fold music floweth,
From the root
Drawn in the dark,
Up to the fruit,
Creeping under the fragrant bark,
Liquid gold, honeysweet thro' and thro'.
Keen-eyed Sisters, singing airily,
Looking warily
Every way,
Guard the apple night and day,
Lest one from the East come and take it away.

II

Father Hesper, Father Hesper, watch, watch, ever
    and aye,
Looking under silver hair with a silver eye.

Poems, 1833

Father, twinkle not thy stedfast sight;
Kingdoms lapse, and climates change, and races die;
Honour comes with mystery;
Hoarded wisdom brings delight.
Number, tell them over and number
How many the mystic fruit-tree holds,
Lest the redcombed dragon slumber
Rolled together in purple folds.
Look to him, father, lest he wink, and the golden apple be stol'n away,
For his ancient heart is drunk with overwatchings night and day,
Round about the hallowed fruit tree curled—
Sing away, sing aloud and evermore in the wind, without stop,
Lest his scalèd eyelid drop,
For he is older than the world.
If he waken, we waken,
Rapidly levelling eager eyes.
If he sleep, we sleep,
Dropping the eyelid over the eyes.
If the golden apple be taken
The world will be overwise.
Five links, a golden chain, are we,
Hesper, the dragon, and sisters three,
Bound about the golden tree

Poems, 1833

III

Father Hesper, Father Hesper, watch, watch, night
 and day,
Lest the old wound of the world be healèd,
The glory unsealèd,
The golden apple stol'n away,
And the ancient secret revealèd.
Look from west to east along:
Father, old Himla weakens, Caucasus is bold and
 strong.
Wandering waters unto wandering waters call;
Let them clash together, foam and fall.
Out of watchings, out of wiles,
Comes the bliss of secret smiles,
All things are not told to all,
Half round the mantling night is drawn,
Purplefringed with even and dawn.
Hesper hateth Phosphor, evening hateth morn.

IV

Every flower and every fruit the redolent breath
Of this warm seawind ripeneth,
Arching the billow in his sleep;
But the land-wind wandereth,
Broken by the highland-steep,
Two streams upon the violet deep:
For the western sun and the western star,
And the low west wind, breathing afar,

Poems, 1833

The end of day and beginning of night
Make the apple holy and bright,
Holy and bright, round and full, bright and blest,
Mellowed in a land of rest ;
Watch it warily day and night ;
All good things are in the west,
Till midnoon the cool east light
Is shut out by the round of the tall hillbrow ;
But when the fullfaced sunset yellowly
Stays on the flowering arch of the bough,
The luscious fruitage clustereth mellowly,
Goldenkernelled, goldencored,
Sunset ripened, above on the tree,
The world is wasted with fire and sword,
But the apple of gold hangs over the sea,
Five links, a golden chain, are we,
Hesper, the dragon, and sisters three,
  Daughters three,
  Bound about
  All round about
The gnarlèd bole of the charmèd tree,
The golden apple, the golden apple, the hallowed
 fruit,
Guard it well, guard it warily,
  Watch it warily,
  Singing airily,
Standing about the charmèd root.

Poems, 1833

XXXIII

Rosalind

My Rosalind, my Rosalind,
Bold, subtle, careless Rosalind,
Is one of those who know no strife
Of inward woe or outward fear;
To whom the slope and stream of life
The life before, the life behind,
In the ear, from far and near,
Chimeth musically clear.
My falconhearted Rosalind
Fullsailed before a vigorous wind,
Is one of those who cannot weep
For others' woes, but overleap
All the petty shocks and fears
That trouble life in early years,
With a flash of frolic scorn
And keen delight, that never falls
Away from freshness, self-upborne
With such gladness, as, whenever
The freshflushing springtime calls
To the flooding waters cool,
Young fishes, on an April morn,

Poems, 1833

Up and down a rapid river,
Leap the little waterfalls
That sing into the pebbled pool.
My happy falcon, Rosalind,
Hath daring fancies of her own,
Fresh as the dawn before the day,
Fresh as the early seasmell blown
Through vineyards from an inland bay
My Rosalind, my Rosalind,
Because no shadow on you falls,
Think you hearts are tennis balls
To play with, wanton Rosalind?

Poems, 1833

XXXIV

Song

Who can say
Why To-day
To-morrow will be yesterday?
Who can tell
Why to smell
The violet, recalls the dewy prime
Of youth and buried time?
The cause is nowhere found in rhyme

Poems, 1833

XXXV

Sonnet

Written on hearing of the outbreak of the Polish Insurrection

Blow ye the trumpet, gather from afar
   The hosts to battle : be not bought and sold.
   Arise, brave Poles, the boldest of the bold ;
Break through your iron shackles—fling them far.
O for those days of Piast, ere the Czar
   Grew to this strength among his deserts cold ;
   When even to Moscow's cupolas were rolled
The growing murmurs of the Polish war !
Now must your noble anger blaze out more
   Than when from Sobieski, clan by clan,
The Moslem myriads fell, and fled before—
   Than when Zamoysky smote the Tartar Khan,
Than earlier, when on the Baltic shore
   Boleslas drove the Pomeranian.

Poems, 1833

XXXVI

O Darling Room *

I

O DARLING room, my heart's delight,
Dear room, the apple of my sight,
With thy two couches soft and white,
There is no room so exquisite,
No little room so warm and bright
Wherein to read, wherein to write.

II

For I the Nonnenwerth have seen,
And Oberwinter's vineyards green,
Musical Lurlei; and between
The hills to Bingen have I been,
Bingen in Darmstadt, where the Rhene
Curves towards Mentz, a woody scene.

III

Yet never did there meet my sight,
In any town, to left or right,
A little room so exquisite,
With two such couches soft and white;
Not any room so warm and bright,
Wherein to read, wherein to write.

---

* 'As soon as this poem was published, I altered the second line to "All books and pictures ranged aright"; yet "Dear room, the apple of my sight" (which was much abused) is not as bad as "Do go, dear rain, do go away."' [Note initialed 'A. T.' in *Life*, vol. I, p. 89.] The worthlessness of much of the criticism lavished on Tennyson by his coterie of adulating friends may be judged from the fact that Arthur Hallam wrote to Tennyson that this poem was 'mighty pleasant'

Poems, 1833

XXXVII

To Christopher North

You did late review my lays,
  Crusty Christopher;
You did mingle blame and praise,
  Rusty Christopher.
When I learnt from whom it came,
I forgave you all the blame,
  Musty Christopher;
I could *not* forgive the praise,
  Fusty Christopher.

[This epigram was Tennyson's reply to an article by Professor Wilson—'Christopher North'—in *Blackwood's Magazine* for May 1832, dealing in sensible fashion with Tennyson's 1830 volume, and ridiculing the fulsome praise lavished on him by his inconsiderate friends—especially referring to Arthur Hallam's article in the *Englishman's Magazine* for August, 1831.]

Poems, 1833

XXXVIII

The Lotos-Eaters

[These forty lines formed the conclusion to the original (1833) version of the poem. When the poem was reprinted in the 1842 volumes these lines were suppressed.]

We have had enough of motion,
Weariness and wild alarm,
Tossing on the tossing ocean,
Where the tuskèd seahorse walloweth
In a stripe of grassgreen calm,
At noon-tide beneath the lea;
And the monstrous narwhale swalloweth
His foamfountains in the sea.
Long enough the winedark wave our weary bark did carry.
This is lovelier and sweeter,
Men of Ithaca, this is meeter,
In the hollow rosy vale to tarry,
Like a dreamy Lotos-eater, a delirious Lotos-eater!
We will eat the Lotos, sweet
As the yellow honeycomb,
In the valley some, and some
On the ancient heights divine;

Poems, 1833

And no more roam,
On the loud hoar foam,
To the melancholy home
At the limit of the brine,
The little isle of Ithaca, beneath the day's decline.
We'll lift no more the shattered oar,
No more unfurl the straining sail;
With the blissful Lotos-eaters pale
We will abide in the golden vale
Of the Lotos-land, till the Lotos fail;
We will not wander more.
Hark! how sweet the horned ewes bleat
On the solitary steeps,
And the merry lizard leaps,
And the foam-white waters pour;
And the dark pine weeps,
And the lithe vine creeps,
And the heavy melon sleeps
On the level of the shore:
Oh! islanders of Ithaca, we will not wander more,
Surely, surely, slumber is more sweet than toil, the shore
Than labour in the ocean, and rowing with the oar,
Oh! islanders of Ithaca, we will return no more.

Poems, 1833

XXXIX

A Dream of Fair Women

[In the 1833 volume the poem opened with the following four verses, suppressed after 1842. These Fitz Gerald considered made 'a perfect poem by themselves.']

As when a man, that sails in a balloon,
   Downlooking sees the solid shining ground
Stream from beneath him in the broad blue noon,
   Tilth, hamlet, mead and mound :

And takes his flags and waves them to the mob
   That shout below, all faces turned to where
Glows rubylike the far-up crimson globe,
   Filled with a finer air :

So, lifted high, the poet at his will
   Lets the great world flit from him, seeing all,
Higher thro' secret splendours mounting still,
   Self-poised, nor fears to fall.

Hearing apart the echoes of his fame.
   While I spoke thus, the seedsman, Memory,
Sowed my deep-furrowed thought with many a name
   Whose glory will not die.

Miscellaneous Poems and Contributions to Periodicals
1833-1868

Contributions to Periodicals

XL

Cambridge

[This poem is written in pencil on the fly-leaf of a copy of *Poems* 1833 in the Dyce Collection in South Kensington Museum. Reprinted with many alterations in *Life*, vol. I, p. 67.]

THEREFORE your halls, your ancient colleges,
    Your portals statued with old kings and queens,
Your bridges and your busted libraries,
    Wax-lighted chapels and rich carved screens,
    Your doctors and your proctors and your deans
Shall not avail you when the day-beam sports
    New-risen o'er awakened Albion—No,
    Nor yet your solemn organ-pipes that blow
Melodious thunders through your vacant courts
At morn and even ; for your manner sorts
    Not with this age, nor with the thoughts that roll,
Because the words of little children preach
Against you,—ye that did profess to teach
    And have taught nothing, feeding on the soul.

Miscellaneous Poems and

XLI

The Germ of 'Maud'

[There was published in 1837 in *The Tribute*, (a collection of original poems by various authors, edited by Lord Northampton), a contribution by Tennyson entitled 'Stanzas,' consisting of xvi stanzas of varying lengths (110 lines in all). In 1855 the first xii stanzas were published as the fourth section of the second part of 'Maud.' Some verbal changes and transpositions of lines were made; a new stanza (the present sixth) and several new lines were introduced, and the xth stanza of 1837 became the xiiith of 1855. But stanzas xiii-xvi of 1837 have never been reprinted in any edition of Tennyson's works, though quoted in whole or part in various critical studies of the poet. Swinburne refers to this poem as 'the poem of deepest charm and fullest delight of pathos and melody ever written, even by Mr Tennyson.' This poem in *The Tribute* gained Tennyson his first notice in the *Edinburgh Review*, which had till then ignored him.]

XIII

BUT she tarries in her place
And I paint the beauteous face
    Of the maiden, that I lost,
        In my inner eyes again,
Lest my heart be overborne,
By the thing I hold in scorn,
    By a dull mechanic ghost
        And a juggle of the brain.

Contributions to Periodicals

XIV

I can shadow forth my bride
    As I knew her fair and kind
        As I woo'd her for my wife;
She is lovely by my side
        In the silence of my life—
'Tis a phantom of the mind.

XV

'Tis a phantom fair and good
I can call it to my side,
        So to guard my life from ill,
Tho' its ghastly sister glide
        And be moved around me still
With the moving of the blood
    That is moved not of the will.

XVI

Let it pass, the dreary brow,
    Let the dismal face go by,
Will it lead me to the grave?
    Then I lose it: it will fly:
Can it overlast the nerves?
    Can it overlive the eye?
But the other, like a star,
Thro' the channel windeth far
    Till it fade and fail and die,
To its Archetype that waits
Clad in light by golden gates,
Clad in light the Spirit waits
    To embrace me in the sky.

Miscellaneous Poems and

XLII

[On the fly-leaf of a book illustrated by Bewick, in the library of the late Lord Ravensworth, the following lines in Tennyson's autograph were discovered in 1903.]

A GATE and a field half ploughed,
A solitary cow,
A child with a broken slate,
And a titmarsh in the bough.
But where, alack, is Bewick
To tell the meaning now?

Contributions to Periodicals

XLIII

The Skipping-Rope

[This poem, published in the second volume of *Poems by Alfred Tennyson* (in two volumes, London, Edward Moxon, MDCCCXLII), was reprinted in every edition until 1851, when it was suppressed.]

SURE never yet was Antelope
  Could skip so lightly by.
Stand off, or else my skipping-rope
  Will hit you in the eye.
How lightly whirls the skipping-rope!
  How fairy-like you fly!
Go, get you gone, you muse and mope—
  I hate that silly sigh.
Nay, dearest, teach me how to hope,
  Or tell me how to die.
There, take it, take my skipping-rope
  And hang yourself thereby.

XLIV

The New Timon and the Poets

[From *Punch*, February 28, 1846. Bulwer Lytton published in 1845 his satirical poem 'New Timon: a Romance of London,' in which he bitterly attacked Tennyson for the civil list pension granted the previous year, particularly referring to the poem 'O Darling Room' in the 1833 volume. Tennyson replied in the following vigorous verses, which made the literary sensation of the year. Tennyson afterwards declared: 'I never sent my lines to *Punch*. John Forster did They were too bitter. I do not think that I should ever have published them.'—*Life*, vol. I, p. 245.]

We know him, out of Shakespeare's art,
   And those fine curses which he spoke;
The old Timon, with his noble heart,
   That, strongly loathing, greatly broke.

So died the Old: here comes the New:
   Regard him: a familiar face:
I *thought* we knew him: What, it's you
   The padded man—that wears the stays—

Who killed the girls and thrill'd the boys
   With dandy pathos when you wrote,
A Lion, you, that made a noise,
   And shook a mane en papillotes.

Contributions to Periodicals

And once you tried the Muses too :
  You fail'd, Sir : therefore now you turn
You fall on those who are to you
  As captain is to subaltern.

But men of long enduring hopes,
  And careless what this hour may bring,
Can pardon little would-be Popes
  And Brummels, when they try to sting.

An artist, Sir, should rest in art,
  And wave a little of his claim ;
To have the deep poetic heart
  Is more than all poetic fame.

But you, Sir, you are hard to please ;
  You never look but half content :
Nor like a gentleman at ease
  With moral breadth of temperament.

And what with spites and what with fears,
  You cannot let a body be :
It's always ringing in your ears,
  'They call this man as good as *me*.'

What profits now to understand
  The merits of a spotless shirt—
A dapper boot—a little hand—
  If half the little soul is dirt ?

Miscellaneous Poems and

You talk of tinsel ! why we see
  The old mark of rouge upon your cheeks
You prate of nature ! you are he
  That spilt his life about the cliques.

A Timon you ! Nay, nay, for shame :
  It looks too arrogant a jest—
The fierce old man—to take *his* name
  You bandbox. Off, and let him rest.

Contributions to Periodicals

XLV

Mablethorpe

[Published in *Manchester Athenæum Album*, 1850
 Written, 1837. Republished, altered, in *Life*, vol
 I, p. 161.]

How often, when a child I lay reclined,
 I took delight in this locality!
Here stood the infant Ilion of the mind,
 And here the Grecian ships did seem to be.

And here again I come and only find
 The drain-cut levels of the marshy lea,—
Gray sand banks and pale sunsets—dreary wind,
 Dim shores, dense rains, and heavy clouded sea

Miscellaneous Poems and

XLVI

[Published in *The Keepsake for* 1851: *an illustrated annual*, edited by Miss Power. London : David Bogue. To this issue of the *Keepsake* Tennyson also contributed 'Come not when I am dead' now included in the collected Works.]

WHAT time I wasted youthful hours
One of the shining wingèd powers,
Show'd me vast cliffs with crown of towers,

As towards the gracious light I bow'd,
They seem'd high palaces and proud,
Hid now and then with sliding cloud.

He said, 'The labour is not small ;
Yet winds the pathway free to all :—
Take care thou dost not fear to fall !'

Contributions to Periodicals

XLVII

Britons, Guard your Own

[Published in *The Examiner*, January 31, 1852. Verses 1 (considerably altered), 7, 8 and 10, are reprinted in *Life*, vol. I, p. 344.]

RISE, Britons, rise, if manhood be not dead ;
The world's last tempest darkens overhead ;
    The Pope has bless'd him ;
    The Church caress'd him ;
He triumphs ; maybe, we shall stand alone :
    Britons, guard your own.

His ruthless host is bought with plunder'd gold,
By lying priest's the peasant's votes controlled.
    All freedom vanish'd,
    The true men banished,
He triumphs ; maybe, we shall stand alone.
    Britons, guard your own.

Peace-lovers we—sweet Peace we all desire—
Peace-lovers we—but who can trust a liar ?—
    Peace-lovers, haters
    Of shameless traitors,
We hate not France, but this man's heart of stone.
    Britons, guard your own.

Miscellaneous Poems and

We hate not France, but France has lost her voice
This man is France, the man they call her choice.
      By tricks and spying,
      By craft and lying,
And murder was her freedom overthrown.
      Britons, guard your own.

'Vive l'Empereur' may follow by and bye;
'God save the Queen' is here a truer cry.
      God save the Nation,
      The toleration,
And the free speech that makes a Briton known.
      Britons, guard your own.

Rome's dearest daughter now is captive France,
The Jesuit laughs, and reckoning on his chance,
      Would, unrelenting,
      Kill all dissenting,
Till we were left to fight for truth alone.
      Britons, guard your own.

Call home your ships across Biscayan tides,
To blow the battle from their oaken sides.
      Why waste they yonder
      Their idle thunder?
Why stay they there to guard a foreign throne?
      Seamen, guard your own.

Contributions to Periodicals

We were the best of marksmen long ago,
We won old battles with our strength, the bow.
      Now practise, yeomen,
      Like those bowmen,
Till your balls fly as their true shafts have flown
      Yeomen, guard your own.

His soldier-ridden Highness might incline
To take Sardinia, Belgium, or the Rhine:
      Shall we stand idle,
      Nor seek to bridle
His vile aggressions, till we stand alone?
      Make their cause your own.

Should he land here, and for one hour prevail,
There must no man go back to bear the tale:
      No man to bear it—
      Swear it! We swear it!
Although we fought the banded world alone,
      We swear to guard our own.

Miscellaneous Poems and

XLVIII

Hands all Round

[Published in *The Examiner*, February 7, 1852. Reprinted, slightly altered, in *Life*, vol. I, p. 345. Included, almost entirely re-written, in collected Works.]

First drink a health, this solemn night,
  A health to England, every guest;
That man's the best cosmopolite
  Who loves his native country best.
May Freedom's oak for ever live
  With stronger life from day to day;
That man's the best Conservative
  Who lops the mouldered branch away.
      Hands all round!
  God the tyrant's hope confound!
To this great cause of Freedom drink, my friends,
  And the great name of England round and round.

A health to Europe's honest men!
  Heaven guard them from her tyrants' jails!
From wronged Poerio's noisome den,
  From iron limbs and tortured nails!
We curse the crimes of Southern kings,
  The Russian whips and Austrian rods—
We likewise have our evil things;
  Too much we make our Ledgers, Gods.
      Yet hands all round!

Contributions to Periodicals

    God the tyrant's cause confound!
To Europe's better health we drink, my friends,
    And the great name of England round and round.

What health to France, if France be she
    Whom martial progress only charms?
Yet tell her—better to be free
    Than vanquish all the world in arms.
Her frantic city's flashing heats
    But fire, to blast the hopes of men.
Why change the titles of your streets?
    You fools, you'll want them all again.
        Hands all round!
    God the tyrant's cause confound!
To France, the wiser France, we drink, my friends,
    And the great name of England round and round.

Gigantic daughter of the West,
    We drink to thee across the flood,
We know thee most, we love thee best,
    For art thou not of British blood?
Should war's mad blast again be blown,
    Permit not thou the tyrant powers
To fight thy mother here alone,
    But let thy broadsides roar with ours.
        Hands all round!

Miscellaneous Poems and

    God the tyrant's cause confound!
To our great kinsmen of the West, my friends,
    And the great name of England round and round.

O rise, our strong Atlantic sons,
    When war against our freedom springs!
O speak to Europe through your guns!
    They *can* be understood by kings.
You must not mix our Queen with those
    That wish to keep their people fools;
Our freedom's foemen are her foes,
    She comprehends the race she rules.
        Hands all round!
    God the tyrant's cause confound!
To our dear kinsmen of the West, my friends,
    And the great name of England round and round.

# Contributions to Periodicals

XLIX

Suggested by Reading an Article in a Newspaper

[Published in *The Examiner*, February 14, 1852, and never reprinted nor acknowledged. The proof sheets of the poem, with alterations in Tennyson's autograph, were offered for public sale in 1906.]

To the Editor of *The Examiner*.

SIR,—I have read with much interest the poems of Merlin. The enclosed is longer than either of those, and certainly not so good: yet as I flatter myself that it has a smack of Merlin's style in it, and as I feel that it expresses forcibly enough some of the feelings of our time, perhaps you may be induced to admit it.

TALIESSEN.

How much I love this writer's manly style!
   By such men led, our press had ever been
The public conscience of our noble isle,
   Severe and quick to feel a civic sin,
To raise the people and chastise the times
With such a heat as lives in great creative rhymes.

O you, the Press! what good from you might spring!
   What power is yours to blast a cause or bless!
I fear for you, as for some youthful king,
   Lest you go wrong from power in excess.
Take heed of your wide privileges! we
The thinking men of England, loathe a tyranny.

A freeman is, I doubt not, freest here;
  The single voice may speak his mind aloud;
An honest isolation need not fear
  The Court, the Church, the Parliament, the
    crowd.
No, nor the Press! and look you well to that—
We must not dread in you the nameless autocrat.

And you, dark Senate of the public pen,
  You may not, like yon tyrant, deal in spies.
Yours are the public acts of public men,
  But yours are not their household privacies.
I grant you one of the great Powers on earth,
But be not you the blatant traitors of the hearth.

You hide the hand that writes: it must be so,
  For better so you fight for public ends;
But some you strike can scarce return the blow;
  You should be all the nobler, O my friends.
Be noble, you! nor work with faction's tools
To charm a lower sphere of fulminating fools.

But knowing all your power to heat or cool,
  To soothe a civic wound or keep it raw,
Be loyal, if you wish for wholesome rule:
  Our ancient boast is this—we reverence law.
We still were loyal in our wildest fights,
Or loyally disloyal battled for our rights.

Contributions to Periodicals

O Grief and Shame if while I preach of laws
   Whereby to guard our Freedom from offence—
And trust an ancient manhood and the cause
   Of England and her health of commonsense—
There hang within the heavens a dark disgrace,
Some vast Assyrian doom to burst upon our race.

I feel the thousand cankers of our State,
   I fain would shake their triple-folded ease,
The hogs who can believe in nothing great,
   Sneering bedridden in the down of Peace
Over their scrips and shares, their meats and wine,
With stony smirks at all things human and
     divine!

I honour much, I say, this man's appeal.
   We drag so deep in our commercial mire,
We move so far from greatness, that I feel
   Exception'd to be character'd in fire.
Who looks for Godlike greatness here shall see
The British Goddess, sleek Respectability.

Alas for her and all her small delights!
   She feels not how the social frame is rack'd.
She loves a little scandal which excites;
   A little feeling is a want of tact.
For her there lie in wait millions of foes,
And yet the 'not too much' is all the rule she
     knows.

Miscellaneous Poems and

Poor soul! behold her: what decorous calm!
  She, with her week-day worldliness sufficed,
Stands in her pew and hums her decent psalm
  With decent dippings at the name of Christ!
And she has mov'd in that smooth way so long,
She hardly can believe that she shall suffer wrong.

Alas, our Church! alas, her growing ills,
  And those who tolerate not her tolerance,
But needs must sell the burthen of their wills
  To that half-pagan harlot kept by France!
Free subjects of the kindliest of all thrones,
Headlong they plunge their doubts among old rags and bones.

Alas, Church writers, altercating tribes—
  The vessel and your Church may sink in storms.
Christ cried: Woe, woe, to Pharisees and Scribes!
  Like them, you bicker less for truth than forms.
I sorrow when I read the things you write,
What unheroic pertness! what un-Christian spite!

Alas, our youth, so clever yet so small,
  Thin dilletanti deep in nature's plan,
Who make the emphatic One, by whom is all,
  An essence less concentred than a man!
Better wild Mahmoud's war-cry once again!
O fools, we want a manlike God and Godlike men!

Contributions to Periodicals

Go, frightful omens.   Yet once more I turn
   To you that mould men's thoughts; I call
     on you
To make opinion warlike, lest we learn
   A sharper lesson than we ever knew.
I hear a thunder though the skies are fair,
But shrill you, loud and long, the warning-note:
     Prepare!

Miscellaneous Poems and

L

[Lord Tennyson wrote, by Royal request, two stanzas which were sung as part of *God Save the Queen* at a State concert in connection with the Princess Royal's marriage: these were printed in the *Times* of January 26, 1858.]

GOD bless our Prince and Bride!
God keep their lands allied,
   God save the Queen!
Clothe them with righteousness,
Crown them with happiness,
Them with all blessings bless,
   God save the Queen.

Fair fall this hallow'd hour,
Farewell our England's flower,
   God save the Queen!
Farewell, fair rose of May!
Let both the peoples say,
God bless thy marriage-day,
   God bless the Queen.

Contributions to Periodicals

LI

The Ringlet

[Published in *Enoch Arden* volume (London: E. Moxon & Co, 1864) and never reprinted.]

'Your ringlets, your ringlets,
  That look so golden-gay,
If you will give me one, but one,
  To kiss it night and day,
Then never chilling touch of Time
  Will turn it silver-gray;
And then shall I know it is all true gold
To flame and sparkle and stream as of old,
Till all the comets in heaven are cold,
  And all her stars decay.'
'Then take it, love, and put it by;
This cannot change, nor yet can I.'

'My ringlet, my ringlet,
  That art so golden-gay,
Now never chilling touch of Time
  Can turn thee silver-gray;
And a lad may wink, and a girl may hint,
  And a fool may say his say;

Miscellaneous Poems and

For my doubts and fears were all amiss,
And I swear henceforth by this and this
That a doubt will only come for a kiss,
    And a fear to be kissed away.'
'Then kiss it, love, and put it by:
If this can change, why so can I.'

O Ringlet, O Ringlet,
    I kiss'd you night and day,
And Ringlet, O Ringlet,
    You still are golden-gay,
But Ringlet, O Ringlet,
    You should be silver-gray:
For what is this which now I'm told,
I that took you for true gold,
She that gave you 's bought and sold,
    Sold, sold.

O Ringlet, O Ringlet,
    She blush'd a rosy red,
When Ringlet, O Ringlet,
    She clipt you from her head,
And Ringlet, O Ringlet,
    She gave you me, and said,
'Come, kiss it, love, and put it by:
If this can change, why so can I.'
O fie, you golden nothing, fie
    You golden lie.

Contributions to Periodicals

O Ringlet, O Ringlet,
   I count you much to blame,
For Ringlet, O Ringlet,
   You put me much to shame,
So Ringlet, O Ringlet,
   I doom you to the flame.
For what is this which now I learn,
Has given all my faith a turn?
Burn, you glossy heretic, burn,
        Burn, burn.

Miscellaneous Poems and

LII

Song

[This first form of the Song in *The Princess* ('Home they brought her warrior dead') was published only in *Selections from Tennyson*. London: E. Moxon & Co, 1864.]

    HOME they brought him slain with spears.
        They brought him home at even-fall:
    All alone she sits and hears
        Echoes in his empty hall,
            Sounding on the morrow.

    The Sun peeped in from open field,
        The boy began to leap and prance,
        Rode upon his father's lance,
    Beat upon his father's shield—
            'Oh hush, my joy, my sorrow.'

Contributions to Periodicals

LIII

1865—1866

[Published in *Good Words* for March 1, 1868 as a decorative page, with an accompanying full page plate by T. Dalziel. The lines were never reprinted.]

I STOOD on a tower in the wet,
And New Year and Old Year met,
And winds were roaring and blowing;
And I said, 'O years that meet in tears,
Have ye aught that is worth the knowing?

'Science enough and exploring
Wanderers coming and going
Matter enough for deploring
But aught that is worth the knowing?'

Seas at my feet were flowing
Waves on the shingle pouring,
Old Year roaring and blowing
And New Year blowing and roaring.

The Lover's Tale
1833

[It was originally intended by Tennyson that this poem should form part of his 1833 volume. It was put in type and, according to custom, copies were distributed among his friends, when, on the eve of publication, he decided to omit it. Again, in 1869, it was sent to press with a new third part added, and was again withdrawn, the third part only—'The Golden Supper,' founded on a story in Boccaccio's *Decameron*—being published in the volume, 'The Holy Grail.' In 1866, 1870 and 1875, attempts had been made by Mr Herne Shepherd to publish editions of 'The Lover's Tale,' reprinted from stray proof copies of the 1833 printing. Each of these attempts was repressed by Tennyson, and at last in 1879 the complete poem, as now included in the collected Works, was issued, with an apologetic reference to the necessity of reprinting the poem to prevent its circulation in an unauthorised form. But the 1879 issue is considerably altered from the original issue of 1833, as written by Tennyson in his nineteenth year. Since only as a product of Tennyson's youth does the poem merit any attention, it has seemed good to reprint it here as originally written.]

The Lover's Tale

A FRAGMENT

The Poem of the Lover's Tale (the lover is supposed to be himself a poet) was written in my nineteenth year, and consequently contains nearly as many faults as words. That I deemed it not wholly unoriginal is my only apology for its publication—an apology lame and poor, and somewhat impertinent to boot: so that if its infirmities meet with more laughter than charity in the world, I shall not raise my voice in its defence. I am aware how deficient the Poem is in point of art, and it is not without considerable misgivings that I have ventured to publish even this fragment of it. 'Enough,' says the old proverb, 'is as good as a feast.'—(Tennyson's original introductory note.)

HERE far away, seen from the topmost cliff,
Filling with purple gloom the vacancies
Between the tufted hills the sloping seas
Hung in mid-heaven, and half-way down rare sails,
White as white clouds, floated from sky to sky.
Oh! pleasant breast of waters, quiet bay,
Like to a quiet mind in the loud world,
Where the chafed breakers of the outer sea
Sunk powerless, even as anger falls aside,
And withers on the breast of peaceful love,
Thou didst receive that belt of pines, that fledged
The hills that watch'd thee, as Love watcheth
    Love,—

The Lover's Tale

In thine own essence, and delight thyself
To make it wholly thine on sunny days.
Keep thou thy name of 'Lover's bay': See, Sirs,
Even now the Goddess of the Past, that takes
The heart, and sometimes toucheth but one string
That quivers, and is silent, and sometimes
Sweeps suddenly all its half-moulder'd chords
To an old melody, begins to play
On those first-moved fibres of the brain.
I come, Great mistress of the ear and eye:
Oh! lead me tenderly, for fear the mind
Rain thro' my sight, and strangling sorrow weigh
Mine utterance with lameness.   Tho' long years
Have hallowed out a valley and a gulf
Betwixt the native land of Love and me,
Breathe but a little on me, and the sail
Will draw me to the rising of the sun,
The lucid chambers of the morning star,
And East of life.
              Permit me, friend, I prithee,
To pass my hand across my brows, and muse
On those dear hills, that nevermore will meet
The sight that throbs and aches beneath my touch
As tho' there beat a heart in either eye;
For when the outer lights are darken'd thus,
The memory's vision hath a keener edge.
It grows upon me now—the semicircle
Of dark blue waters and the narrow fringe
Of curving beach—its wreaths of dripping green—
Its pale pink shells—the summer-house aloft

The Lover's Tale

That open'd on the pines with doors of glass,
A mountain nest the pleasure boat that rock'd
Light-green with its own shadow, keel to keel,
Upon the crispings of the dappled waves
That blanched upon its side.

                      O Love, O Hope,
They come, they crowd upon me all at once,
Moved from the cloud of unforgotten things,
That sometimes on the horizon of the mind
Lies folded—often sweeps athwart in storm—
They flash across the darkness of my brain,
The many pleasant days, the moolit nights,
The dewy dawnings and the amber eyes,
When thou and I, Camilla, thou and I
Were borne about the bay, or safely moor'd
Beneath some low brow'd cavern, where the wave
Plash'd sapping its worn ribs (the while without,
And close above us, sang the wind-tost pine,
And shook its earthly socket, for we heard,
In rising and in falling with the tide,
Close by our ears, the huge roots strain and creak),
Eye feeding upon eye with deep intent;
And mine, with love too high to be express'd
Arrested in its sphere, and ceasing from
All contemplation of all forms, did pause
To worship mine own image, laved in light,
The centre of the splendours, all unworthy
Of such a shrine—mine image in her eyes,

The Lover's Tale

By diminution made most glorious,
Moved with their motions, as those eyes were
    moved
With motions of the soul, as my heart beat
Twice to the melody of hers. Her face
Was starry-fair, not pale, tenderly flush'd
As 'twere with dawn. She was dark-hair'd, dark-
    eyed ;
Oh, such dark eyes ! A single glance of them
Will govern a whole life from birth to death,
Careless of all things else, led on with light
In trances and in visions : look at them,
You lose yourself in utter ignorance,
You cannot find their depth ; for they go back,
And farther back, and still withdraw themselves
Quite into the deep soul, that evermore,
Fresh springing from her fountains in the brain,
Still pouring thro', floods with redundant light
Her narrow portals.

                   Trust me, long ago
I should have died, if it were possible
To die in gazing on that perfectness
Which I do bear within me ; I had died
But from my farthest lapse, my latest ebb,
Thine image, like a charm of light and strength
Upon the waters, pushed me back again
On these deserted sands of barren life.
Tho' from the deep vault, where the heart of
    hope

The Lover's Tale

Fell into dust, and crumbled in the dark—
Forgetting who to render beautiful
Her countenance with quick and healthful blood—
Thou didst not sway me upward, could I perish
With such a costly casket in the grasp
Of memory ? He, that saith it, hath o'erstepp'd
The slippery footing of his narrow wit,
And fall'n away from judgment. Thou art light
To which my spirit leaneth all her flowers,
And length of days, and immortality
Of thought, and freshness ever self-renew'd.
For Time and Grief abode too long with Life,
And like all other friends i' the world, at last
They grew aweary of her fellowship :
So Time and Grief did beckon unto Death,
And Death drew nigh and beat the doors of Life
But thou didst sit alone in the inner house,
A wakeful port'ress and didst parle with Death,
'This is a charmed dwelling which I hold' ;
So Death gave back, and would no further come.
Yet is my life nor in the present time,
Nor in the present place. To me alone,
Pushed from his chair of regal heritage,
The Present is the vassal of the Past :
So that, in that I *have* lived, do I live,
And cannot die, and am, in having been,
A portion of the pleasant yesterday,
Thrust forward on to-day and out of place ;
A body journeying onward, sick with toil,
The lithe limbs bow'd as with a heavy weight

The Lover's Tale

And all the senses weaken'd in all save that
Which, long ago, they had glean'd and garner'd up
Into the granaries of memory—
The clear brow, bulwark of the precious brain,
Now seam'd and chink'd with years—and all the
  while
The light soul twines and mingles with the
  growths
Of vigorous early days, attracted, won,
Married, made one with, molten into all
The beautiful in Past of act or place.
Even as the all-enduring camel, driven
Far from the diamond fountain by the palms,
Toils onward thro' the middle moonlight nights,
Shadow'd and crimson'd with the drifting dust,
Or when the white heats of the blinding noons
Beat from the concave sand ; yet in him keeps
A draught of that sweet fountain that he loves,
To stay his feet from falling, and his spirit
From bitterness of death.

                      Ye ask me, friends,
When I began to love.   How should I tell ye ?
Or from the after fulness of my heart,
Flow back again unto my slender spring
And first of love, tho' every turn and depth
Between is clearer in my life than all
Its present flow.   Ye know not what ye ask.
How should the broad and open flower tell
What sort of bud it was, when press'd together

The Lover's Tale

In its green sheath, close lapt in silken folds?
It seemed to keep its sweetness to itself,
Yet was not the less sweet for that it seem'd.
For young Life knows not when young Life was born,
But takes it all for granted: neither Love,
Warm in the heart, his cradle can remember
Love in the womb, but resteth satisfied,
Looking on her that brought him to the light:
Or as men know not when they fall asleep
Into delicious dreams, our other life,
So know I not when I began to love.
This is my sum of knowledge—that my love
Grew with myself—and say rather, was my growth,
My inward sap, the hold I have on earth,
My outward circling air wherein I breathe,
Which yet upholds my life, and evermore
Was to me daily life and daily death:
For how should I have lived and not have loved?
Can ye take off the sweetness from the flower,
The colour and the sweetness from the rose,
And place them by themselves? or set apart
Their motions and their brightness from the stars,
And then point out the flower or the star?
Or build a wall betwixt my life and love,
And tell me where I am? 'Tis even thus:
In that I live I love; because I love
I live: whate'er is fountain to the one
Is fountain to the other; and whene'er

The Lover's Tale

Our God unknits the riddle of the one,
There is no shade or fold of mystery
Swathing the other.

                  Many, many years,
For they seem many and my most of life,
And well I could have linger'd in that porch,
So unproportioned to the dwelling place,
In the maydews of childhood, opposite
The flush and dawn of youth, we lived together,
Apart, alone together on those hills.
Before he saw my day my father died,
And he was happy that he saw it not:
But I and the first daisy on his grave
From the same clay came into light at once.
As Love and I do number equal years
So she, my love, is of an age with me.
How like each other was the birth of each!
The sister of my mother—she that bore
Camilla close beneath her beating heart,
Which to the imprisoned spirit of the child,
With its true touched pulses in the flow
And hourly visitation of the blood,
Sent notes of preparation manifold,
And mellow'd echoes of the outer world—
My mother's sister, mother of my love,
Who had a twofold claim upon my heart,
One twofold mightier than the other was,
In giving so much beauty to the world,
And so much wealth as God had charged her with

The Lover's Tale

Loathing to put it from herself for ever,
Crown'd with her highest act the placid face
And breathless body of her good deeds past.
So we were born, so orphan'd. She was motherless,
And I without a father. So from each
Of those two pillars which from earth uphold
Our childhood, one had fall'n away, and all
The careful burthen of our tender years
Trembled upon the other. He that gave
Her life, to me delightedly fulfill'd
All loving-kindnesses, all offices
Of watchful care and trembling tenderness.
He worked for both : he pray'd for both : he slept
Dreaming of both ; nor was his love the less
Because it was divided, and shot forth
Boughs on each side, laden with wholesome shade,
Wherein we rested sleeping or awake,
And sung aloud the matin-song of life.

She was my foster-sister : on one arm
The flaxen ringlets of our infancies
Wander'd, the while we rested : one soft lap
Pillow'd us both : one common light of eyes
Was on us as we lay : our baby lips,
Kissing one bosom, ever drew from thence
The stream of life, one stream, one life, one blood,
One sustenance, which, still as thought grew large,
Still larger moulding all the house of thought,
Perchance assimilated all our tastes

The Lover's Tale

And future fancies.   'Tis a beautiful
And pleasant meditation, what whate'er
Our general mother meant for me alone,
Our mutual mother dealt to both of us :
So what was earliest mine in earliest life,
I shared with her in whom myself remains.
As was our childhood, so our infancy,
They tell me, was a very miracle
Of fellow-feeling and communion.
They tell me that we would not be alone,—
We cried when we were parted ; when I wept,
Her smile lit up the rainbow on my tears,
Stay'd on the clouds of sorrow ; that we loved
The sound of one another's voices more
Than the grey cuckoo loves his name, and learn'd
To lisp in tune together ; that we slept
In the same cradle always, face to face,
Heart beating time to heart, lip pressing lip,
Folding each other, breathing on each other,
Dreaming together (dreaming of each other
They should have added) till the morning light
Sloped thro' the pines, upon the dewy pane
Falling, unseal'd our eyelids, and we woke
To gaze upon each other.   If this be true,
At thought of which my whole soul languishes
And faints, and hath no pulse, no breath, as tho'
A man in some still garden should infuse
Rich attar in the bosom of the rose,
Till, drunk with its own wine and overfull
Of sweetness, and in smelling of itself,

The Lover's Tale

It fall on its own thorns—if this be true—
And that way my wish leaneth evermore
Still to believe it—'tis so sweet a thought,
Why in the utter stillness of the soul
Doth question'd memory answer not, nor tell,
Of this our earliest, our closest drawn,
Most loveliest, most delicious union?
Oh, happy, happy outset of my days!
Green springtide, April promise, glad new year
Of Being, which with earliest violets,
And lavish carol of clear-throated larks,
Fill'd all the march of life.—I will not speak of thee;
These have not seen thee, these can never know thee,
They cannot understand me. Pass on then
A term of eighteen years. Ye would but laugh
If I should tell ye how I heard in thought
Those rhymes, 'The Lion and the Unicorn'
'The Four-and-twenty Blackbirds' 'Banbury Cross,'
'The Gander' and 'The man of Mitylene,'
And all the quaint old scraps of ancient crones,
Which are as gems set in my memory,
Because she learn'd them with me. Or what profits it
To tell ye that her father died, just ere
The daffodil was blown; or how we found
The drowned seaman on the shore? These things
Unto the quiet daylight of your minds

The Lover's Tale

Are cloud and smoke, but in the dark of mine
Show traced with flame. Move with me to that hour,
Which was the hinge on which the door of Hope,
Once turning, open'd far into the outward,
And never closed again.

                I well remember,
It was a glorious morning, such a one
As dawns but once a season. Mercury
On such a morning would have flung himself
From cloud to cloud, and swum with balanced wings
To some tall mountain. On that day the year
First felt his youth and strength, and from his spring
Moved smiling toward his summer. On that day,
Love working shook his wings (that charged the winds
With spiced May-sweets from bound to bound) and blew
Fresh fire into the sun, and from within
Burst thro' the heated buds, and sent his soul
Into the songs of birds, and touch'd far-off
His mountain-altars, his high hills, with flame
Milder and purer. Up the rocks we wound;
The great pine shook with lovely sounds of joy,
That came on the sea-wind. As mountain brooks
Our blood ran free: the sunshine seem'd to brood

The Lover's Tale

More warmly on the heart than on the brow.
We often paused, and looking back, we saw
The clefts and openings in the hills all fill'd
With the blue valley and the glistening brooks,
And with the low dark groves—a land of Love;
Where Love was worshipp'd upon every height,
Where Love was worshipp'd under every tree—
A land of promise, flowing with the milk
And honey of delicious memories
Down to the sea, as far as eye could ken,
From verge to verge it was a holy land,
Still growing holier as you near'd the bay,
For where the temple stood. When we had reach'd
The grassy platform on some hill, I stoop'd,
I gather'd the wild herbs, and for her brows
And mine wove chaplets of the self-same flower,
Which she took smiling, and with my work there
Crown'd her clear forehead. Once or twice she told me
(For I remember all things), to let grow
The flowers that run poison in their veins.
She said, 'The evil flourish in the world';
Then playfully she gave herself the lie:
'Nothing in nature is unbeautiful,
So, brother, pluck and spare not.' So I wove
Even the dull-blooded poppy, 'whose red flower
Hued with the scarlet of a fierce sunrise,
Like to the wild youth of an evil king,
Is without sweetness, but who crowns himself

The Lover's Tale

Above the secret poisons of his heart
In his old age '—a graceful thought of hers
Graven on my fancy ! As I said, with these
She crown'd her forehead. O how like a nymph,
A stately mountain-nymph, she look'd ! how native
Unto the hills she trod on ! What an angel !
How clothed with beams ! My eyes, fix'd upon hers,
Almost forgot even to move again.
My spirit leap'd as with those thrills of bliss
That shoot across the soul in prayer, and show us
That we are surely heard. Methought a light
Burst from the garland I had woven, and stood
A solid glory on her bright black hair :
A light, methought, broke from her dark, dark eyes,
And shot itself intothe singing winds ;
A light, methought, flash'd even from her white robe,
As from a glass in the sun, and fell about
My footsteps on the mountains.

      About sunset
We came unto the hill of woe, so call'd
Because the legend ran that, long time since,
One rainy night, when every wind blew loud,
A woful man had thrust his wife and child
With shouts from off the bridge, and following, plunged
Into the dizzy chasm below. Below,

The Lover's Tale

Sheer thro' the black-wall'd cliff the rapid brook
Shot down his inner thunders, built above
With matted bramble and the shining gloss
Of ivy-leaves, whose low-hung tresses, dipp'd
In the fierce stream, bore downward with the wave.
The path was steep and loosely strewn with crags
We mounted slowly : yet to both of us
It was delight, not hindrance : unto both
Delight from hardship to be overcome,
And scorn of perilous seeming : unto me
Intense delight and rapture that I breathed,
As with a sense of nigher Deity,
With her to whom all outward fairest things
Were by the busy mind referr'd, compared,
As bearing no essential fruits of excellence.
Save as they were the types and shadowings
Of hers—and then that I became to her
A tutelary angel as she rose,
And with a fearful self-impelling joy
Saw round her feet the country far away,
Beyond the nearest mountain's bosky brows,
Burst into open prospect—heath and hill,
And hollow lined and wooded to the lips—
And steep down walls of battlemented rock
Girded with broom or shiver'd into peaks—
And glory of broad waters interfused,
Whence rose as it were breath and steam of gold ;
And over all the great wood rioting
And climbing, starr'd at slender intervals
With blossom tufts of purest white ; and last,

The Lover's Tale

Framing the mighty landskip to the West,
A purple range of purple cones, between
Whose interspaces gush'd, in blinding bursts,
The incorporate light of sun and sea.

                At length,
Upon the tremulous bridge, that from beneath
Seemed with a cobweb firmament to link
The earthquake-shattered chasm, hung with shrubs,
We passed with tears of rapture. All the West,
And even unto the middle South, was ribb'd
And barr'd with bloom on bloom. The sun beneath,
Held for a space 'twixt cloud and wave, shower'd down
Rays of a mighty circle, weaving over
That varied wilderness a tissue of light
Unparallel'd. On the other side the moon,
Half-melted into thin blue air, stood still
And pale and fibrous as a wither'd leaf,
Nor yet endured in presence of his eyes
To imbue his lustre; most unloverlike;
Since in his absence full of light and joy
And giving light to others. But this chiefest,
Next to her presence whom I loved so well,
Spoke loudly, even into my inmost heart,
As to my outward hearing: the loud stream,
Forth issuing from his portals in the crag
(A visible link unto the home of my heart),
Ran amber toward the West, and nigh the sea,

The Lover's Tale

Parting my own loved mountains, was received
Shorn of its strength, into the sympathy
Of that small bay, which into open main
Glow'd intermingling close beneath the sun
Spirit of Love! That little hour was bound,
Shut in from Time, and dedicate to thee;
Thy fires from heav'n had touch'd it, and the earth
They fell on became hallow'd evermore.

We turn'd: our eyes met: her's were bright, and mine
Were dim with floating tears, that shot the sunset,
In light rings round me; and my name was borne
Upon her breath. Henceforth my name has been
A hallow'd memory, like the names of old;
A center'd, glory-circled memory,
And a peculiar treasure, brooking not
Exchange or currency; and in that hour
A hope flow'd round me, like a golden mist
Charm'd amid eddies of melodious airs,
A moment, ere the onward whirlwind shatter it,
Waver'd and floated—which was less than Hope,
Because it lack'd the power of perfect Hope;
But which was more and higher than all Hope,
Because all other Hope hath lower aim;
Even that this name to which her seraph lips
Did lend such gentle utterance, this one name
In some obscure hereafter, might inwreathe

The Lover's Tale

(How lovelier, nobler then !) her life, her love,
With my life, love, soul, spirit and heart and
    strength.

'Brother,' she said, 'let this be call'd henceforth
The Hill of Hope'; and I replied: 'O sister,
My will is one with thine; the Hill of Hope.'
Nevertheless, we did not change the name.

Love lieth deep; Love dwells not in lip-depths:
Love wraps her wings on either side the heart,
Constraining it with kisses close and warm,
Absorbing all the incense of sweet thoughts
So that they pass not to the shrine of sound.
Else had the life of that delighted hour
Drunk in the largeness of the utterance
Of Love; but how should earthly measure mete
The heavenly unmeasured or unlimited Love,
Which scarce can tune his high majestic sense
Unto the thunder-song that wheels the spheres;
Scarce living in the Æolian harmony,
And flowing odour of the spacious air;
Scarce housed in the circle of this earth:
Be cabin'd up in words and syllables,
Which waste with the breath that made 'em.
                          Sooner earth
Might go round heaven, and the straight girth of
    Time
Inswathe the fullness of Eternity,
Than language grasp the infinite of Love.

The Lover's Tale

O day, which did enwomb that happy hour,
Thou art blest in the years, divinest day!
O Genius of that hour which dost uphold
Thy coronal of glory like a God,
Amid thy melancholy mates far-seen,
Who walk before thee, and whose eyes are dim
With gazing on the light and depth of thine
Thy name is ever worshipp'd among hours!
Had I died then, I had not seem'd to die
For bliss stood round me like the lights of heaven,
That cannot fade, they are so burning bright.
Had I died then, I had not known the death;
Planting my feet against this mound of time
I had thrown me on the vast, and from this impulse
Continuing and gathering ever, ever,
Agglomerated swiftness, I had lived
That intense moment thro' eternity.
Oh, had the Power from whose right hand the light
Of Life issueth, and from whose left hand floweth
The shadow of Death, perennial effluences,
Whereof to all that draw the wholesome air,
Somewhile the one must overflow the other;
Then had he stemm'd my day with night and driven
My current to the fountain whence it sprang—
Even his own abiding excellence—
On me, methinks, that shock of gloom had fall'n
Unfelt, and like the sun I gazed upon,

The Lover's Tale

Which, lapt in seeming dissolution,
And dipping his head low beneath the verge,
Yet bearing round about him his own day,
In confidence of unabated strength,
Steppeth from heaven to heaven, from light to
    light,
And holding his undimmed forehead far
Into a clearer zenith, pure of cloud ;
So bearing on thro' Being limitless
The triumph of this foretaste, I had merged
Glory in glory, without sense of change.

We trod the shadow of the downward hill ;
We pass'd from light to dark. On the other side
Is scooped a cavern and a mountain-hall,
Which none have fathom'd. If you go far in
(The country people rumour) you may hear
The moaning of the woman and the child,
Shut in the secret chambers of the rock.
I too have heard a sound—perchance of streams
Running far-off within its inmost halls,
The home of darkness, but the cavern mouth,
Half overtrailed with a wanton weed
Gives birth to a brawling stream, that stepping
    lightly
Adown a natural stair of tangled roots,
Is presently received in a sweet grove
Of eglantine, a place of burial
Far lovelier than its cradle ; for unseen
But taken with the sweetness of the place,

The Lover's Tale

It giveth out a constant melody
That drowns the nearer echoes.   Lower down
Spreads out a little lake, that, flooding, makes
Cushions of yellow sand ; and from the woods
That belt it rise three dark tall cypresses ;
Three cypresses, symbols of mortal woe,
That men plant over graves.

      Hither we came,
And sitting down upon the golden moss
Held converse sweet and low—low converse sweet
In which our voices bore least part.   The wind
Told a love-tale beside us, how he woo'd
The waters, and the crisp'd waters lisp'd
The kisses of the wind, that, sick with love,
Fainted at intervals, and grew again
To utterance of passion.   Ye cannot shape
Fancy so fair as is this memory.
Methought all excellence that ever was
Had drawn herself from many thousand years,
And all the separate Edens of this earth,
To centre in this place and time.   I listen'd,
And her words stole with most prevailing sweet-
  ness
Into my heart, as thronged fancies come,
All unawares, into the poet's brain ;
Or as the dew-drops on the petal hung,
When summer winds break their soft sleep with
  sighs,
Creep down into the bottom of the flower.

The Lover's Tale

Her words were like a coronal of wild blooms
Strung in the very negligence of Art,
Or in the art of Nature, where each rose
Doth faint upon the bosom of the other,
Flooding its angry cheek with odorous tears.
So each with each inwoven lived with each,
And were in union more than double-sweet.
What marvel my Camilla told me all?
It was so happy an hour, so sweet a place,
And I was as the brother of her blood,
And by that name was wont to live in her speech,
Dear name! which had too much of nearness in it
And heralded the distance of this time.
At first her voice was very sweet and low,
As tho' she were afeard of utterance;
But in the onward current of her speech,
(As echoes of the hollow-banked brooks
Are fashioned by the channel which they keep)
His words did of their meaning borrow sound,
Her cheek did catch the colour of her words,
I heard and trembled, yet I could but hear;
My heart paused,—my raised eyelids would not fall,
But still I kept my eyes upon the sky.
I seem'd the only part of Time stood still,
And saw the motion of all other things;
While her words, syllable by syllable,
Like water, drop by drop, upon my ear
Fell, and I wish'd, yet wish'd her not to speak,

The Lover's Tale

But she spoke on, for I did name no wish.
What marvel my Camilla told me all
Her maiden dignities of Hope and Love,
'Perchance' she said 'return'd.' Even then the
    stars
Did tremble in their stations as I gazed;
But she spake on, for I did name no wish,
No wish—no hope. Hope was not wholly dead,
But breathing hard at the approach of Death,
Updrawn in expectation of her change—
Camilla, my Camilla, who was mine
No longer in the dearest use of mine—
The written secrets of her inmost soul
Lay like an open scroll before my view,
And my eyes read, they read aright, her heart
Was Lionel's: it seem'd as tho' a link
Of some light chain within my inmost frame
Was riven in twain: that life I heeded not
Flow'd from me, and the darkness of the grave,
The darkness of the grave and utter night,
Did swallow up my vision: at her feet,
Even the feet of her I loved, I fell,
Smit with exceeding sorrow unto death.

Then had the earth beneath me yawning given
Sign of convulsion; and tho' horrid rifts
Sent up the moaning of unhappy spirits
Imprison'd in her centre, with the heat
Of their infolding element; had the angels,
The watchers at heaven's gate, push'd them apart,

The Lover's Tale

And from the golden threshold had down-roll'd
Their heaviest thunder, I had lain as still,
And blind and motionless as then I lay !
White as quench'd ashes, cold as were the hopes
Of my lorn love ! What happy air shall woo.'
The wither'd leaf fall'n in the woods, or blasted
Upon this bough ? a lightning stroke had come
Even from that Heaven in whose light I bloom'd
And taken away the greenness of my life,
The blossom and the fragrance. Who was cursed
But I ? who miserable but I ? even Misery
Forgot herself in that extreme distress,
And with the overdoing of her part
Did fall away into oblivion.
The night in pity took away my day
Because my grief as yet was newly born,
Of too weak eyes to look upon the light,
And with the hasty notice of the ear,
Frail life was startled from the tender love
Of him she brooded over. Would I had lain
Until the pleached ivy tress had wound
Round my worn limbs, and the wild briar had
    driven
Its knotted thorns thro' my unpaining brows
Leaning its roses on my faded eyes.
The wind had blown above me, and the rain
Had fall'n upon me, and the gilded snake
Had nestled in this bosomthrone of love,
But I had been at rest for evermore.

The Lover's Tale

Long time entrancement held me : all too soon,
Life (like a wanton too-officious friend
Who will not hear denial, vain and rude
With proffer of unwished for services)
Entering all the avenues of sense,
Pass'd thro' into his citadel, the brain
With hated warmth of apprehensiveness :
And first the chillness of the mountain stream
Smote on my brow, and then I seem'd to hear
Its murmur, as the drowning seaman hears,
Who with his head below the surface dropt,
Listens the dreadful murmur indistinct
Of the confused seas, and knoweth not
Beyond the sound he lists : and then came in
O'erhead the white light of the weary moon,
Diffused and molten into flaky cloud.
Was my sight drunk, that it did shape to me
Him who should own that name ? or had my fancy
So lethargised discernment in the sense,
That she did act the step-dame to mine eyes,
Warping their nature, till they minister'd
Unto her swift conceits ? 'Twere better thus
If so be that the memory of that sound
With mighty evocation, had updrawn
The fashion and the phantasm of the form
It should attach to. There was no such thing.—
It was the man she loved, even Lionel,
The lover Lionel, the happy Lionel,
All joy ; who drew the happy atmosphere

The Lover's Tale

Of my unhappy sighs, fed with my tears,
To him the honey dews of orient hope.
Oh ! rather had some loathly ghastful brow,
Half-bursten from the shroud, in cere cloth bound,
The dead skin withering on the fretted bone,
The very spirit of Paleness made still paler
By the shuddering moonlight, fix'd his eyes on mine
Horrible with the anger and the heat
Of the remorseful soul alive within,
And damn'd unto his loathed tenement.
Methinks I could have sooner met that gaze !
Oh, how her choice did leap forth from his eyes !
Oh, how her love did clothe itself in smiles
About his lips ! This was the very arch-mock
And insolence of uncontrolled Fate,
When the effect weigh'd seas upon my head
To twit me with the cause.

                Why how was this ?
Could he not walk what paths he chose, nor breathe
What airs he pleased ! Was not the wide world free,
With all her interchange of hill and plain
To him as well as me ? I know not, faith :
But Misery, like a fretful, wayward child,
Refused to look his author in the face,
Must he come my way too ? Was not the South,
The East, the West, all open, if he had fall'n
In love in twilight ? Why should he come my way,

The Lover's Tale

Robed in those robes of light I must not wear,
With that great crown of beams about his brows ?
Come like an angel to a damned soul ?
To tell him of the bliss he had with God ;
Come like a careless and a greedy heir,
That scarce can wait the reading of the will
Before he takes possession ? Was mine a mood
To be invaded rudely, and not rather
A sacred, secret, unapproached woe
Unspeakable ? I was shut up with grief ;
She took the body of my past delight,
Narded, and swathed and balm'd it for herself,
And laid it in a new-hewn sepulchre,
Where man had never lain. I was led mute
Into her temple like a sacrifice ;
I was the high-priest in her holiest place,
Not to be loudly broken in upon.
Oh ! friend, thoughts deep and heavy as these well-nigh
O'erbore the limits of my brain ; but he
Bent o'er me, and my neck his arm upstay'd
From earth. I thought it was an adder's fold,
And once I strove to disengage myself,
But fail'd, I was so feeble. She was there too :
She bent above me too : her cheek was pale,
Oh ! very fair and pale : rare pity had stolen
The living bloom away, as tho' a red rose
Should change into a white one suddenly.
Her eyes, I saw, were full of tears in the morn,
And some few drops of that distressful rain

The Lover's Tale

Being wafted on the wind, drove in my sight,
And being there they did break forth afresh
In a new birth, immingled with my own,
And still bewept my grief. Keeping unchanged
The purport of their coinage. Her long ringlets,
Drooping and beaten with the plaining wind,
Did brush my forehead in their to-and-fro :
For in the sudden anguish of her heart
Loosed from their simple thrall they had flowed
    abroad,
And onward floating in a full, dark wave,
Parted on either side her argent neck,
Mantling her form half way. She, when I woke,
After my refluent health made tender quest
Unanswer'd, for I spoke not : for the sound
Of that dear voice so musically low,
And now first heard with any sense of pain,
As it had taken life away before,
Choked all the syllables that in my throat
Strove to uprise, laden with mournful thanks,
From my full heart : and ever since that hour,
My voice hath somewhat falter'd — and what
    wonder
That when hope died, part of her eloquence
Died with her ? He, the blissful lover, too,
From his great hoard of happiness distill'd
Some drops of solace ; like a vain rich man,
That, having always prosper'd in the world,
Folding his hands deals comfortable words
To hearts wounded for ever ; yet, in truth,

The Lover's Tale

Fair speech was his and delicate of phrase,
Falling in whispers on the sense, address'd
More to the inward than the outward ear,
As rain of the midsummer midnight soft
Scarce-heard, recalling fragrance and the green
Of the dead spring—such as in other minds
Had film'd the margents of the recent wound.
And why was I to darken their pure love,
If, as I knew, they two did love each other,
Because my own was darken'd? Why was I
To stand within the level of their hopes,
Because my hope was widow'd, like the cur
In the child's adage? Did I love Camilla?
Ye know that I did love her: to this present
My full-orb'd love hath waned not. Did I love
  her,
And could I look upon her tearful eyes?
Tears wept for me; for me—weep at my grief?
What had *she* done to weep—let my heart
Break rather—whom the gentlest airs of heaven
Should kiss with an unwonted gentleness.
Her love did murder mine; what then? she
  deem'd
I wore a brother's mind: she call'd me brother:
She told me all her love: she shall not weep.

The brightness of a burning thought awhile
Battailing with the glooms of my dark will,
Moonlike emerged, lit up unto itself,
Upon the depths of an unfathom'd woe,

The Lover's Tale

Reflex of action, starting up at once,
As men do from a vague and horrid dream,
And throwing by all consciousness of self,
In eager haste I shook him by the hand;
Then flinging myself down upon my knees
Even where the grass was warm where I had lain,
I pray'd aloud to God that he would hold
The hand of blessing over Lionel,
And her whom he would make his wedded wife,
Camilla! May their days be golden days,
And their long life a dream of linked love,
From which may rude Death never startle them,
But grow upon them like a glorious vision
Of unconceived and awful happiness,
Solemn but splendid, full of shapes and sounds,
Swallowing its precedent in victory.
Let them so love that men and boys may say,
Lo! how they love each other! till their love
Shall ripen to a proverb unto all,
Known when their faces are forgot in the land.
And as for me, Camilla, as for me,
Think not thy tears will make my name grow green,—
The dew of tears is an unwholesome dew.
The course of Hope is dried,—the life o' the plant—
They will but sicken the sick plant more.
Deem then I love thee but as brothers do,
So shalt thou love me still as sisters do;
Or if thou dream'st aught farther, dream but how

The Lover's Tale

I could have loved thee, had there been none else
To love as lovers, loved again by thee.

Or this, or somewhat like to this, I spoke,
When I did see her weep so ruefully;
For sure my love should ne'er induce the front
And mask of Hate, whom woful ailments
Of unavailing tears and heart deep moans
Feed and envenom, as the milky blood
Of hateful herbs a subtle-fanged snake.
Shall Love pledge Hatred in her bitter draughts,
And batten on his poisons? Love forbid!
Love passeth not the threshold of cold Hate,
And Hate is strange beneath the roof of Love.
O Love, if thou be'st Love, dry up these tears
Shed for the love of Love; for tho' mine image,
The subject of thy power, be cold in her,
Yet, like cold snow, it melteth in the source
Of these sad tears, and feeds their downward flow.
So Love, arraign'd to judgment and to death,
Received unto himself a part of blame.
Being guiltless, as an innocent prisoner,
Who when the woful sentence hath been past,
And all the clearness of his fame hath gone
Beneath the shadow of the curse of men,
First falls asleep in swoon. Wherefrom awaked
And looking round upon his tearful friends,
Forthwith and in his agony conceives
A shameful sense as of a cleaving crime—
For whence without some guilt should such grief be?

The Lover's Tale

So died that hour, and fell into the abysm
Of forms outworn, but not to be outworn,
Who never hail'd another worth the Life
That made it sensible.   So died that hour,
Like odour wrapt into the winged wind
Borne into alien lands and far away.
There be some hearts so airy-fashioned,
That in the death of love, if e'er they loved,
On that sharp ridge of utmost doom ride highly
Above the perilous seas of change and chance ;
Nay, more, holds out the lights of cheerfulness ;
As the tall ship, that many a dreary year
Knit to some dismal sandbank far at sea,
All through the lifelong hours of utter dark,
Showers slanting light upon the dolorous wave.
For me all other Hopes did sway from that
Which hung the frailest : falling, they fell too,
Crush'd link on link into the beaten earth,
And Love did walk with banish'd Hope no more,
It was ill-done to part ye, Sisters fair ;
Love's arms were wreathed about the neck of Hope,
And Hope kiss'd Love, and Love drew in her breath
In thât close kiss, and drank her whisper'd tales.
They said that Love would die when Hope was
     gone,
And Love mourned long, and sorrowed after Hope;
At last she sought out memory, and they trod
The same old paths where Love had walked with
     Hope,
And Memory fed the soul of Love with tears.

The Lover's Tale

II

From that time forth I would not see her more,
But many weary moons I lived alone—
Alone, and in the heart of the great forest.
Sometimes upon the hills beside the sea
All day I watched the floating isles of shade,
And sometimes on the shore, upon the sands
Insensibly I drew her name, until
The meaning of the letters shot into
My brain : anon the wanton billow wash'd
Them over, till they faded like my love.
The hollow caverns heard me—the black brooks
Of the mid-forest heard me—the soft winds,
Laden with thistledown and seeds of flowers,
Paused in their course to hear me, for my voice
Was all of thee : the merry linnet knew me,
The squirrel knew me, and the dragon-fly
Shot by me like a flash of purple fire.
The rough briar tore my bleeding palms; the hemlock,
Brow high, did strike my forehead as I pas'd ;
Yet trod I not the wild-flower in my path,
Nor bruised the wild-bird's egg.
                              Was this the end ?
Why grew we then together i' the same plot ?
Why fed we the same fountain ? drew the same sun ?
Why were our mothers branches of one stem ?
Why were we one in all things, save in that

The Lover's Tale

Where to have been one had been the roof and
    crown
Of all I hoped and fear'd ? if that same nearness
Were father to this distance, and that *one*
Vauntcourier this *double ?* If affection
Living slew Love, and Sympathy hew'd out
The bosom-sepulchre of Sympathy.

Chiefly I sought the cavern and the hill
Where last we roam'd together, for the sound
Of the loud stream was pleasant, and the wind
Came wooingly with violet smells. Sometimes
All day I sat within the cavern-mouth,
Fixing my eyes on those three cypress-cones
Which spired above the wood ; and with mad
    hand
Tearing the bright leaves of the ivy-screen,
I cast them in the noisy brook beneath,
And watch'd them till they vanished from my
    sight
Beneath the bower of wreathed eglantines :
And all the fragments of the living rock,
(Huge splinters, which the sap of earliest showers,
Or moisture of the vapour, left in clinging,
When the shrill storm-blast feeds it from behind,
And scatters it before, had shatter'd from
The mountain, till they fell, and with the shock
Half dug their own graves), in mine agony,
Did I make bear of all the deep rich moss
Wherewith the dashing runnel in the spring

The Lover's Tale

Had liveried them all over. In my brain
The spirit seem'd to flag from thought to thought,
Like moonlight wandering through a mist: my blood
Crept like the drains of a marsh thro' all my body;
The motions of my heart seem'd far within me,
Unfrequent, low, as tho' it told its pulses;
And yet it shook me, that my frame did shudder,
As it were drawn asunder by the rack.
But over the deep graves of Hope and Fear,
The wreck of ruin'd life and shatter'd thought,
Brooded one master-passion evermore,
Like to a low hung and a fiery sky
Above some great metropolis, earth shock'd
Hung round with ragged-rimmed burning folds,
Embathing all with wild and woful hues—
Great hills of ruins, and collapsed masses
Of thunder-shaken columns, indistinct
And fused together in the tyrannous light.

So gazed I on the ruins of that thought
Which was the playmate of my youth—for which
I lived and breathed: the dew, the sun, the rain,
Unto the growth of body and of mind;
The blood, the breath, the feeling and the motion,
The slope into the current of my years,
Which drove them onward—made them sensible;
The precious jewel of my honour'd life,
Erewhile close couch'd in golden happiness,
Now proved counterfeit, was shaken out,
And, trampled on, left to its own decay.

The Lover's Tale

Sometimes I thought Camilla was no more,
Some one had told me she was dead, and ask'd me
If I would see her burial : then I seem'd
To rise, and thro' the forest-shadow borne
With more than mortal swiftness, I ran down
The steepy sea-bank, till I came upon
The rear of a procession, curving round
The silver-sheeted bay : in front of which
Six stately virgins, all in white, upbare
A broad earth-sweeping pall of whitest lawn,
Wreathed round the bier with garlands : in the distance,
From out the yellow woods, upon the hill,
Look'd forth the summit and the pinnacles
Of a grey steeple. All the pageantry,
Save those six virgins which upheld the bier,
Were stoled from head to foot in flowing black ;
One walk'd abreast with me, and veiled his brow,
And he was loud in weeping and in praise
Of the departed : a strong sympathy
Shook all my soul : I flung myself upon him
In tears and cries : I told him all my love,
How I had loved her from the first ; whereat
He shrunk and howl'd, and from his brow drew back
His hand to push me from him ; and the face
The very face and form of Lionel,
Flash'd through my eyes into my innermost brain,
And at his feet I seemed to faint and fall,
To fall and die away. I could not rise,

The Lover's Tale

Albeit I strove to follow. They pass'd on,
The lordly Phantasms; in their floating folds
They pass'd and were no more: but I had fall'n
Prone by the dashing runnel on the grass.

Always th' inaudible, invisible thought
Artificer and subject, lord and slave
Shaped by the audible and visible,
Moulded the audible and visible;
All crisped sounds of wave, and leaf and wind,
Flatter'd the fancy of my fading brain;
The storm-pavilion'd element, the wood,
The mountain, the three cypresses, the cave,
Were wrought into the tissue of my dream.
The moanings in the forest, the loud stream,
Awoke me not, but were a part of sleep;
And voices in the distance, calling to me,
And in my vision bidding me dream on,
Like sounds within the twilight realms of dreams,
Which wander round the bases of the hills,
And murmur in the low-dropt eaves of sleep,
But faint within the portals. Oftentimes
The vision had fair prelude, in the end
Opening on darkness, stately vestibules
To cares and shows of Death; whether the mind,
With a revenge even to itself unknown,
Made strange division of its suffering
With her, whom to have suffering view'd had been
Extremest pain; or that the clear-eyed Spirit,

The Lover's Tale

Being blasted in the Present, grew at length
Prophetical and prescient of whate'er
The Future had in store ; or that which most
Enchains belief, the sorrow of my spirit
Was of so wide a compass it took in
All I had loved, and my dull agony,
Ideally to her transferred, became
Anguish intolerable.
     The day waned ;
Alone I sat with her : about my brow
Her warm breath floated in the utterance
Of silver-chorded tones : her lips were sunder'd
With smiles of tranquil bliss, which broke in light
Like morning from her eyes—her eloquent eyes
(As I have seen them many hundred times),
Fill'd all with clear pure fire, thro' mine down
 rain'd
Their spirit-searching splendours. As a vision
Unto a haggard prisoner, iron-stay'd
In damp and dismal dungeons underground
Confined on points of faith, when strength is
 shock'd
With torment, and expectancy of worse
Upon the morrow, thro' the ragged walls,
All unawares before his half-shut eyes,
Comes in upon him in the dead of night,
And with th' excess of sweetness and of awe,
Makes the heart tremble, and the eyes run over
Upon his steely gyves ; so those fair eyes
Shone on my darkness forms which ever stood

The Lover's Tale

Within the magic cirque of memory,
Invisible but deathless, waiting still
The edict of the will to reassume
The semblance of those rare realities
Of which they were the mirrors.   Now the light,
Which was their life, burst through the cloud
    of thought
Keen, irrepressible.
                    It was a room
Within the summer-house of which I spoke,
Hung round with paintings of the sea, and one
A vessel in mid-ocean, her heaved prow
Clambering, the mast bent, and the revin wind
In her sail roaring.   From the outer day,
Betwixt the closest ivies came a broad
And solid beam of isolated light,
Crowded with driving atomies, and fell
Slanting upon that picture, from prime youth
Well-known, well-loved.   She drew it long ago
Forth gazing on the waste and open sea,
One morning when the upblown billow ran
Shoreward beneath red clouds, and I had pour'd
Into the shadowing pencil's naked forms
Colour and life : it was a bond and seal
Of friendship, spoken of with tearful smiles ;
A monument of childhood and of love,
The poesy of childhood ; my lost love
Symbol'd in storm.   We gazed on it together
In mute and glad remembrance, and each heart
Grew closer to the other, and the eye

The Lover's Tale

Was riveted and charm-bound, gazing like
The Indian on a still-eyed snake, low crouch'd
A beauty which is death, when all at once
That painted vessel, as with inner life,
'Gan rock and heave upon that painted sea;
An earthquake, my loud heartbeats, made the ground
Roll under us, and all at once soul, life,
And breath, and motion, pass'd and flow'd away
To those unreal billows: round and round
A whirlwind caught and bore us; mighty gyves,
Rapid and vast, of hissing spray wind-driven
Far through the dizzy dark. Aloud she shriek'd—
My heart was cloven with pain. I wound my arms
About her: we whirl'd giddily: the wind
Sung: but I clasp'd her without fear: her weight
Shrank in my grasp, and over my dim eyes
And parted lips which drank her breath, down hung
The jaws of Death: I, screaming, from me flung
The empty phantom: all the sway and whirl
Of the storm dropt to windless calm, and I
Down welter'd thro' the dark ever and ever.

Index to First Lines

	Page
A gate and a field half ploughed	92
All thoughts, all creeds, all dreams, are true	55
Angels have talked with him and showed him thrones	33
As when a man, that sails in a balloon	85
Blow ye the trumpets, gather from afar	80
But she tarries in her place	90
Check every outflash, every ruder sally	65
Could I outwear my present state of woe	44
Ere yet my heart was sweet Love's tomb	37
Every day hath its night	29
First drink a health, this solemn night	102
God bless our Prince and Bride	110
Heaven weeps above the earth all night	41
Here far away, seen from the topmost cliff	119
His eyes in eclipse	25
Home they brought him slain with spears	114
How much I love this writer's manly style	105
How often, when a child I lay reclined	97
I am any man's suitor	23
I stood on a tower in the wet	115
I stood upon the Mountain which o'erlooks	11
I' the glooming light	28
Me my own fate to lasting sorrow doometh	66
My Rosalind, my Rosalind	77
O darling room, my heart's delight	81
Oh, Beauty, passing beauty! sweetest sweet!	71
Oh, go not yet, my love	31
O maiden fresher than the first green leaf	42

Index to First Lines

	Page
O sad *No more*! O sweet *No more*	64
O thou whose fringèd lids I gaze upon	43
Rise, Britons, rise, if manhood be not dead	99
Sainted Juliet! dearest name	27
Shall the hag Evil die with the child of Good	46
Sure never yet was Antelope	93
The lintwhite and the throstlecock	56
The Northwind fall'n in the new starred night	72
The pallid thunderstricken sigh for gain	47
There are three things that fill my heart with sighs	67
Therefore your halls, your ancient colleges	89
There is no land like England	52
The varied earth, the moving heaven	38
Thou, from the first, unborn, undying love	48
Though Night hath climbed her peak	45
Two bees within a chrystal flowerbell rockèd	54
Voice of the summerwind	35
We have had enough of motion	83
We know him, out of Shakespeare's art	94
What time I wasted youthful hours	98
Where is the Giant of the Sun, which stood	61
Who can say	79
Who fears to die? Who fears to die	50
With roses musky breathed	63
You cast to ground the hope which once was mine	40
You did late review my lays	82
Your ringlets, your ringlets	111

www.ingramcontent.com/pod-product-compliance
Lightning Source LLC
Chambersburg PA
CBHW011342090426
42743CB00018B/3416